SHINWELL
TALKING

A Conversational Biography to Celebrate
his hundredth birthday

JOHN DOXAT

Quiller Press
London

SHINWELL TALKING

Dedication

This book can only be dedicated to
the subject of it, a nobleman —
also a noble man — Manny

First published 1984 by
Quiller Press Ltd
50 Albemarle Street
London W1X 4BD

Design and production in association with
Book Production Consultants, 47 Norfolk Street, Cambridge CB1 2LE

Printed by The Burlington Press (Cambridge) Ltd,
Foxton, Cambridge CB2 6SW

ISBN 0 907621 43 0

Contents

An Explanation

Picture two men sitting opposite each other in a cosy room in a quiet Hampstead road. One is nearing seventy: the other is thirty years older — though he does not look so. Occasionally, both light their pipes: they happen to share a preference for the same brand of tobacco. On a table between them, beside an unobtrusive microphone, are a bottle of Scotch whisky, a small water-jug and two cut-glass tumblers. The two men talk — though one mostly listens.

This scene will be repeated, with growing familiarity and cordiality, over several weeks, until twenty-two ninety-minute cassettes are more or less filled. On playback, these tapes will show how truly conversational have been these meetings. They have not been interviews; they are part duologue, part argument of the most amicable, sometimes spontaneous soliloquizing. They have all the virtues of extempore speech, and its failings — the pauses and interruptions.

The older man, the subject, is Emanuel Shinwell, Lord Shinwell, better known affectionately to the public as Manny — highly articulate, never needing to refer to a note or book, with a twinkling humour, speaking without false modesty yet totally lacking vanity, generous of thought, and (sometimes annoyingly to the listener) reluctant to criticize.

The younger man, myself, is as self-effacing as possible, without being over-awed. I must be mildly provocative. What I am searching for is not the material for another formal biography: Manny Shinwell has published his own history, political and personal, in several volumes. It is for a socio–political student one day to write a definitive Life of this remarkable person. I am seeking to create a verbal portrait — a self-portrait. It is to be in Manny's own words. I want to encapsulate the man by invoking his powers of recall, by eavesdropping, as it were, on his thoughts.

* * *

If Manny Shinwell had followed the common habit of allowing ambition to erode principle, he would have undoubtedly been elected leader of his party and probably have become Prime Minister. He preferred the satisfaction of speaking his mind, remaining true to his ideals — heeding changing conditions but scornful of cynical pragmatism — and thus, with integrity intact, after a tumultuous and influential career, he achieved the status of true Elder Statesman.

How unlikely it would have seemed to a Mrs Shinwell, of Dutch—Jewish family, married to a British man with Hebraic—Polish parents, when she gave birth to the first of her thirteen children in teeming, cosmopolitan Spitalfields — that this son would become a Member of Parliament, let alone that he would several times be a Minister of the Crown and eventually a peer of the realm. Yet was not the name of the street in which she lived prophetic: Freeman Street, since vanished like most of the squalid areas of that son's early years? The boy from Freeman Street became a Freeman of the City of London, on whose humble borders he was born, after freeing himself from his disadvantaged circumstances and helping to free many others from the shackles of poverty and despair.

As an appendix to this volume I give an outline of this outstanding self-levitation from privation to Palace of Westminster. It is a fine example of that most popular of all folk-tales — a rise from rags to prosperity, the under-privileged lad making good through his own endeavours. The same energy could make a captain of industry: Manny directed his genius towards what he considered his duty to his fellow-men.

It has been my task to get behind this story, not to re-tell it. By recording some of Manny's views and memories, his reactions to certain events and personalities, I hope to create a picture of the essential man: I reiterate, I present aspects of a larger whole.

Britain has been rich in such characters, men who have hewn their way to the top without any inheritance other than their native wits and a sound constitution. But we have never had one who has lived for so long at the heart of events. There is little merit in great longevity on its own: that may be merely survival. However, there are rich rewards to be gleaned from probing into the accumulated wisdom of an acute mind, first sharpened by adversity, then honed by success, and finally mellowed, yet not diminished, by great age. Manny's basic philosophy may be said to rest on what he calls 'the inevitability of change'. He has seen more changes than most of us — vast material improvements, an element of moral decline, fine social achievements, many aspirations thwarted by human fallibility. He has contributed to these changes, being neither excessively elated by success nor soured by disappointment. He continues to debate not only the broad issues, the 'problems' that constantly occupy him, but the little, individually important matters of daily life — its pleasures as well as its duties.

* * *

Had Boswell had access to modern technology – and had he transcribed literally every exchange with Johnson exactly as spoken by the Doctor — the result would not have been a classic of biographical literature: it would have been barely readable. Boswell's particular genius lay in capturing the essence of Johnson's style, orotund and eccentric, so that the reader feels he is hearing the lexicographer's original speech. Conversation is not oratory. Not even the most fluent of us — thank God — talk in totally grammatical, finely turned periods. We may listen to an actor playing Hamlet and at the time believe that is just how the Prince of Denmark would have spoken — although we know that such poetical dialogue is totally unreal. On a different level, the "verbatim" Hansard Reports of Parliamentary proceedings are liable to substantial editing to make them intelligible.

So, of course, I have edited my tapes. I have omitted hours from them. I have been selective. I have brought into a single section observations on a topic that were made weeks apart. I have disciplined the digressions, repetitions and *non sequiturs* that are happily part of normal social chat: I have not always completed sentences left suspended . . . I have added, in parenthesis, words that could be taken as spoken but which were not in fact uttered. I have also added, in italics, ancillary information I deemed essential, nor have I entirely eschewed occasional comment. I have truncated, or suppressed, a high percentage of my own questions, interpolations, interruptions and expressions of opinion; I have endeavoured to preserve my own contributions to the conversations only so far as to indicate the informal nature of my sessions with Manny and to avoid any impression that they were occupied with monologues or that I was a sycophantic questioner sitting at the feet of the master. There was plenty of give-and-take.

The choice of subjects, especially the emphasis given them, was strictly Manny's. Remember, I was not conducting interviews in the accepted sense. Although I might have tried to turn Manny in a certain direction, I rarely succeeded; to have insisted could have spoiled the ease of our verbal intercourse. Reflected here are events or personalities or ideas about which Manny *wished* to speak. He might choose virtually to make a speech on some topic I found of minor general interest and then dismiss in a sentence a matter on which I would have liked him to wax expansive. So you will find here that several people are not accorded space relative to their perceived importance, or self-importance.

The Personal History items that flow throughout the book illustrate Manny's more intimate life, as opposed to the public man. They are not only extracts from my recordings, but are reinforced by condensations of his own words in autobiographical writings, particularly *Lead With The Left.**

I elected, after considering various methods of presentation, to group main topics under broad alphabetical headings. Whilst compressing much that was diffuse, I hope to have maintained the spontaneity of our exchanges, resisting any temptation to re-cast them in a false literary style. Words attributed to Manny are entirely his own. This *is* Manny Shinwell talking.

J.D.

Lead With the Left: My First Ninety-Six Years; Manny Shinwell, Cassell, London, 1981.

Manny talks about . . .

Ancestry

My father lived until he was ninety-three. He was a difficult man to get on with — very harsh — all right with me but he was cross in his attitude to other members of the family. If he'd been different, we'd have made a fortune. No doubt about it. He wanted everyone to do what he wanted. Had my father been reasonable and got the family to work with him, we'd have made that fortune. When he was doing well, he was indeed doing well. One of his troubles was that he had to wander about. He was never content. He must have been ambitious, trying to do better than he had done. Perhaps that's part of my own character — trying to do better. That is so — because when I do something, like making a speech, I say to myself, 'Oh, dear, I could have done better I'm sure.'

On Being Jewish
J.D. *"Do you have any feelings at all of being Jewish?"*
No, I don't — but the only reservation I make is that I support Israel. But why? Why do I do that? Just now I'm annoyed with them because of the religious element butting in — very angry.

What pleased me was when Israel decided to defend itself. This is part of my character of course. I said in the House of Commons that I gloried in the fact that the Jews were defending themselves. You see, that was my own attitude. I won't allow anyone to injure me — no matter who the person. That the Israelis were ready to fight: that, to me, was everything. But it was the same for any other minority — to fight for themselves: nothing can be more glorious than that. One crowded hour of glorious life . . . *We concluded the well-known lines in unison.*

That is my attitude generally. When I've been chairman of the House of Lords Defence Committee, I wouldn't yield an inch on Defence matters. I don't want war, but the idea of allowing the Russians to put one over on me! Who do they think they are? Could it be that my early life was of such character, with all its strife and tribulations, that I'm trying to make amends for it by hitting out?

J.D. "Isn't it just patriotism — the unfashionable word today? ... Have you ever encountered anti-Semitism?"
Very rarely. *Manny then recalled the incident with Commander Bower.* I had to prove I wasn't a coward.

This was less an instance of overt anti-Semitism as of misplaced chauvinism. In 1938, during Question Time in the Commons, Manny queried the facilities given by the Government to Franco's London agent. Commander Bower, MP for Cleveland, shouted, "Go back to Poland!" Manny crossed the floor and struck him in the face. Afterwards, both men apologized to the Speaker. Some time later, the antagonists were personally reconciled after the Commander, in the Lobby, had congratulated Manny on a speech — much to his surprise.

No, I have no feelings of Jewishness. I don't kid myself about King Solomon and all that. Chosen race? I wish I could say I was one of the Chosen Race: I'd be expecting to do something really phenomenal!

* * *

I am not a practising Jew ...

J.D. "But your family background was Orthodox."
That surprises me. My grandfather was very religious, and my father was a bit — but not very much. But somehow, reading scientific stuff ... I began to have doubts about the whole thing — very strong doubts, as I still do. I am not too dogmatic about it all: I wonder about it all. When I think about that space-probe thing: I wonder where it's gone. It's entered remote space — but what is there? What is matter? What is space?

You come to me with the New Testament, and ask me to accept it — well, well, well ... The Old Testament is a very nice story ... So, because I don't like to offend people, I don't discuss it. But I have my own feelings. Very often, in the middle of the night, I think about these things. I wonder about it all, and wish I could come to some conclusions.

* * *

When my father decided to go back to South Shields — I didn't stay long — and I went back to Glasgow, I never had [much] more contact with Jewish people. [*When a Jewish Clothing Workers' Union was formed, Manny joined another union as he objected to a purely ethnic organization.*| I lived in the Catholic quarter of Glasgow. All my friends were Roman Catholics. My first holiday was with them in Ireland. My brother married a Catholic girl from Londonderry: my father was furious.

Personal History

Father's Side

In 1868, my grandfather brought his family to Britain — symbol of tolerance and freedom for oppressed people. My grandfather was last of a family who had been flour millers |in Poland| for centuries. He was compelled to leave his native village by the occupying Power, Czarist Russia.

He and his family were, in modern jargon, refugees, but they did not arrive helpless and dependent on charity. My grandfather was a miller and master baker. My father was then about seven. From Hull, my grandfather made his way to Leeds where he set up in business. It was said that while its rival, Bradford, was the filthiest town in the country, Leeds had the doubtful distinction of achieving maximum overcrowding.

At the age of ten, my father went to work as errand boy with a tailor. By the age of twelve he was earning 6 shillings a week. One Friday, he took longer than expected on an errand and found the shop closed on his return. His father chastised him for coming home without his wages, being convinced he had spent them. The following Friday, he received two weeks' wages and decided to seek his fortune in London.

His money was just sufficient for a single ticket on a cheap night train. As he wandered about the forecourt of St Pancras, a policeman asked him what he was doing, and roared with laughter when my father told him he had come to London to look for work. He told him how to get to the East End.

An elderly Jew took pity on him, invited him to a meal and found him a job. He stayed in London two years and then returned to Leeds. He again quarrelled with his father, and then went to Glasgow. My grandfather later emigrated to South Africa. My father went again to London, and then to Glasgow. There he organized a strike, which destroyed all chances of getting more work. By the age of eighteen he was back in London, working in the Spitalfields area.

Clement Attlee (Earl Attlee)

Many people supported Attlee on the grounds that he was innocuous. He was anything but spectacular. I knew him quite well because he'd been a member of the Independent Labour Party — he joined after I did — so much so that in 1920, when we had a conference and I was elected chairman of the Standing Orders committee, in charge of resolutions, somebody came to me and asked if I would give him a chance to move his resolution. 'Where are you from?' 'Limehouse,' he said. I didn't know who he was, so I said, 'Look I'll do the best I can for you.' I hadn't even asked him his name. Only later I discovered it was Attlee.

J.D. "He was always referred to as Major Attlee."
Major Attlee with the clipped accent. It happens he becomes leader of the party: he's Prime Minister. Well now, he appoints his government. He sends for me. He says, 'I want you to nationalize the mines, and you'll be in the Cabinet.' Of course, if he hadn't said the Cabinet I wouldn't have looked at it. I said, 'All right,' and he said, 'Go nationalize them.' Just like that. I went back to my office and saw my officials there. I said, 'Have you got any documents?' They'd got nothing there. I said, 'Apply to the Labour Party: there's something by Arthur Greenwood' — who was drunk nearly all the time. I had to provide the evidence for legislation myself, without any consultation.

Conspiracies

Not long afterwards, there was a conspiracy against Attlee. This time |unlike a previous occasion|, Arthur Greenwood wasn't involved directly. They wanted to get Arthur to stand against Attlee. Now the trouble about Arthur was that he was never sober — even when speaking from the front bench. |Sir Robert Bruce| Lockhart, in an article in the *Telegraph* on the return of Labour |in 1945| writes about Greenwood being drunk and about screams coming from the room where he worked, screams — women's screams. I can remember. Greenwood had a room along the corridor in the House of Commons and very often, in passing, you'd hear some shouting going on. On this particular occasion, Lockhart was right: I heard the screams myself . . . He was dismissed from the War Cabinet because of that. He refused to stand against Attlee.

The next conspiracy was when Cripps and Dalton asked Ernie Bevin if he'd stand against Attlee, and Ernie, to his credit, said, 'No, I'll have nothing to do with it.' Now I was aware of these conspiracies — and part of the time Attlee was ill. In fact, he was so ill I went up to St

Mary's Hospital at a time when I thought he wouldn't come out again. But he recovered.

I would say that without Ernie Bevin and the assistance he got from |Herbert| Morrison, although he didn't like Morrison — I couldn't understand his dislike of Morrison and still haven't found out — he never would have been able to carry on.

J.D. "Would anyone else at the time have made a good leader?"
Morrison, in my opinion. Morrison was no use when he became Foreign Secretary, but in my opinion he'd have been a good leader . . . I think he'd have been a good Prime Minister

Attlee, during that period, I would say he must have been awfully ill. Half a dozen times at least. He suffered from eczema very badly, and other troubles. But I tell you what — he was completely under the influence of Ernie Bevin: no question about that.

* * *

|Attlee| was a good chairman of committee — when he was there. He never bothered about taking a vote. He would collect the voices |by asking senior colleagues.| He did that after the war |in Europe| when he was Deputy Leader to Churchill and Churchill wanted to carry on until the Japs had surrendered. We had a |party| meeting in Blackpool to discuss Churchill's letter, and we opposed it. Attlee wanted to carry on until some months later. Bevin wanted the same — and Dalton. Nye Bevan and I were opposed to it. And then Attlee asked Whiteley, the Chief Whip, one of the North-east people and a rough diamond, who said, 'The lads won't have it.' He meant the MPs. Attlee announced next day we'd fight the election.

No "Blackmail"

Lockhart |in his serialized memoirs in the *Telegraph*| talks about that |meeting| — and that's where he requires correction. He writes that when Ernie Bevin had spoken about his idea of a nine months' election postponement, Nye Bevan had jumped up and shouted, 'If you do that, I'll raise the whole country against you!' Then Lockhart says that Ernie Bevin said, 'That's blackmail,' and Nye said, 'Blackmail? You've been blackmailing me for these last three years. You talk about blackmail!'

Now I was there. It's absolutely untrue: not a word of truth in it. He must have asked someone what happened — couldn't have been somebody who was there. The night before |the decision|, I had talked to Nye Bevan, in the Clifton Hotel, Blackpool, about what to do about Morrison. We heard Morrison was on the fence, and we decided to try

to persuade him the next morning, before the meeting, to vote with us —
and he did. All that Bevan said at the meeting was that we shouldn't wait
and see. It was a most harmonious meeting, at which Attlee told us
officially of Churchill's letter.

Regrets About Cabinet Decisions

I am sorry to have to say this. But after long years as a member of a
political party, and in the political life of the country, and having
occupied responsible positions, and having been associated with people
like Attlee, I can't become reconciled to some of the things that
happened. I can't forget Indian self-government, Indian independence,
and the massacres that took place. [That was] badly planned. It was a
matter of impulse with him — something he had to do because he'd been
associated with the Simon Commission on India.

Behaviour

What has worried me for many years has been the deterioration of both
personal and social behaviour. Going back to the beginning of the
century, when I entered public life, although social conditions were far
from satisfactory — vast unemployment, most of it unregistered, no
social security, thousands of people actually starving, maternal mortality
rates very high . . . since then there has undoubtedly been a deterioration
in manners. There is a lack of consideration for other people. We're
pushing each other around far more aggressively than when I was
younger. [Then] if one went on a tram and it was crowded, one would
always make way for one of the female sex, particularly if the person
was somewhat older — sometimes because she was much younger! And
the behaviour of those looking after passengers, collectors and so on —
they were without question better behaved and more considerate than
those now on the buses.

J.D. "To what do you attribute this deterioration primarily?"
There are all sorts of reasons for it. In those days – although, as I've
said, there was excessive poverty and far more ill-health — somehow

people didn't push each other around so much. They did have consideration. If you walked along a street and met someone, the first thing they
would ask was, 'Are you working?' I remember that so well. It wasn't,
'Are you keeping well?' It was, 'Are you working?' Because there was
so much unemployment. People had concern. There was more
neighbourliness amongst the working class than there is now. You
always talked over the garden fence /*a telling criticism of municipal
high-rise flats*/ or stood at the gate. And women would congregate,
especially on washing-days. The water supply was centralized — stand-
pipes — not every house had water piped in. People met, inquired about
each other. Certainly amongst children, manners were — I wouldn't say
impeccable — but far better than nowadays, when children don't seem
to care two hoots for their elders.

J.D. "There was more parental discipline."
That as well. There was another factor. Fewer married women went out
to work. Indeed, working-class fathers were rather humiliated if their
women went to work. Many had to — as cleaners, skivvies, doing
menial tasks. But certainly amongst the artisan class, the idea of a skilled
engineer's wife working was out of the question. That meant children
were better looked after, better disciplined.

People talk about policies — new policies, changing policies about
everything. I attach more importance to behaviour than I do to policy:
far more to that. For example, what happened at the |recent| Labour
Conference? It wasn't policy that mattered: it was attitude.
Brotherhood! The very thing they talked about — Brotherhood! How
do they define that? Let's take an example from Brighton —
Brotherhood . . . hitting each other, cursing each other, ready to indulge
in fisticuffs!

To me, looking at the world as it is — as a person who's been a long
time in politics — you ask yourself, 'What's gone wrong?' Is it politics
have gone wrong? Isn't it BEHAVIOUR?

Take South Africa. Take Russia. It's a matter of behaviour — by
which I mean consideration, to some extent compassion — behaviour.
How one conducts oneself. I apply that |criterion| to the coloured
people. I have no prejudice against coloured people — none at all —
except when a coloured man becomes aggressive. I have the same
feelings with a white man. It's a question of education — and yet you
can have the best education in the world and your behaviour can be
abominable.

I would go so far as to say — and you may think this an exaggeration
— that looking at the world as it is today, the one thing we need above
all else is BETTER BEHAVIOUR.

Manny liked to extemporize on a theme, often mischievously and with an element of hyperbole. Here he concluded with a chuckle:
Having said that, I think we should have a drink.

Tony Benn

Take this fellow, Benn. I don't care tuppence about his changes of policy, his Left-wing ideas. I know what it all means — talk, talk, talk. But when you're endowed with some measure of authority — you do nothing. Even with myself — the very same.

J.D. *"Benn's such an extraordinary case to the average person. Some people say he's a traitor to his class?"*
His father, Wedgie Benn, Viscount Stansgate [the title Tony Benn rejected], was a member of the Cabinet in which I was. He was a member of the Independent Labour Party, after being a Liberal. Who was the grandfather? I remember him years ago. Whenever he made a speech he spoke about Cromwell: always Cromwell. He was a Liberal, a solicitor from Cornwall. We talk about class; he was a solicitor.

J.D. *"What one would call middle class."*
I would say ordinary middle class. His son became a Member of Parliament. He was a proper WASP – Tony Benn's father — always talking. He lost his seat, and when that happened he decided to join the Independent Labour Party. The ILP was the propagandist element of the Labour Party. I was a member. When he joined us, I remember a committee meeting we had. He wanted to become a Parliamentary candidate, and we had a rule you couldn't become a candidate until you had been a member for twelve months. Now they decided, largely because he had some friends on the executive, to allow him [in] six months. I opposed it all the way through on the grounds of principle. I was defeated and he became an MP again. When he was a member of the Lords and in the Cabinet, I can't remember him doing anything special. He was certainly nothing like his son . . .

* * *

None of the ideas which he [Tony Benn] has advocated is new to the

Labour party. It's his attitude [to which I object] — it's a question of behaviour. I watch him very closely on TV, and, of course, when I see him. He's got a sneering attitude, an attitude of contempt for everyone else. I think he wants to be a leader not because he thinks he could do anything, but just because he wants to be leader. *This was said before Benn lost, and regained, a Parliamentary seat. But on a later occasion Manny virtually contradicted this judgement, saying:* Benn, he's troublesome. I don't know that he's so anxious to be leader of the party. I think he wants to be prominent, well-liked, well-known. He has a great deal of satisfaction in having a large number of Members of Parliament behind him, all cheering him on.

James Callaghan

When he was Chancellor of the Exchequer, he sent for me. I wasn't in the government. He was preparing his budget, and he wanted to know what he should do. I said, 'Look here, Jim, the one thing you're not going to do is give me any budget secrets. I'm not taking any chances. Look what happened to Dalton [*forced to resign after inadvertently leaking budget information*]. If you want my opinion — tell the country the truth, and don't be afraid of being unpopular. Tell the truth. There are certain things we [Labour] know we can't do; isn't it about time you told them? You won't suffer.' He agreed with me — but he didn't do it.

The real trouble about Callaghan is he talks an awful lot but he hasn't an awful lot of courage. You have to have more than ability in politics: you have to be firm about things. It doesn't matter a damn if it affects your interests.

* * *

Callaghan came into the House of Commons in 1945, when I was a Cabinet Minister. He'd been in the Navy. When I had nationalized the mines — '46–'47 — I happened to go up to Edinburgh to address a meeting of the Co-Operative Union; I was to speak on industrial democracy.

I warned them, from my experience of nationalization, that before we embarked on any further adventures of that kind we should have a working-party and put out blue-prints to consider the administration, and also the consequences of what we were doing, financial matters . . . otherwise we'd meet with disaster.

I received a letter from Callaghan in which he complained about my attitude and actually said I was doing a disservice to the party. I didn't bother about it. I discussed it with my Parliamentary Private Secretary, Colonel [Lord] Wigg, and he wanted me to publish the letter. But that would have done Callaghan a lot of harm. If I'd showed it to Attlee, he'd have been furious for a member criticizing a Cabinet Minister. So nothing was done — but the threat existed I might publish the letter. And I think that worried Callaghan a bit.

Then he made progress. He made one or two good speeches. Later on he became a junior Minister, and then worked his way up. There are various ways of achieving your ambitions: everybody to his own taste. Eventually, he became Chancellor of the Exchequer, and did one or two things that were quite good. Time went on. Occasionally I would criticize his government: when he became PM, I was in the Lords.

I was friendly with him: it was always Jim and Manny. When he became PM and the troubles occured — unions, wages — I knew he was in difficulties. One day, I said to him, 'We'd better have a talk,' and he arranged I should see him the following week. I wanted to warn him how to deal with this question.

It so happened we had to defer it, and meanwhile he had to make a declaration. He decided on 'the 5 per cent norm'. That's the one thing I wanted to warn him against. I had hinted about it in speeches I was making at that time in the Lords: that you mustn't be too inflexible — you must allow for a certain compromise — discussion — and if I'd met him I would have said, 'If you're going to talk about a norm, talk about any particular figures depending very much on circumstances. It's for the trade unions to make a suggestion. Then wear them down a bit.' If he'd done that, he'd have avoided trouble. Instead, he then did the worst thing he could have done: when the Ford people decided to increase wages by about 16 per cent, he threatened them with sanctions.

No, I don't think he was a great PM. I think Callaghan was, and is, a quite good politician, but not on the highest level. I wouldn't say he was comparable with Wilson. Whatever else may be said about Wilson, he was competent, well-informed. If he made a mistake, he could cover it up. If Callaghan made mistakes, he wasn't able to cover them up. It seemed to me that Callaghan would make a statement but wouldn't allow himself [room] to manoeuvre out of it later. He isn't astute enough for that. You've got to be a bit clever there. He's a normal politician. There were other people in the government who could have made a better job of it. I think Peter Shore could have . . . Healey could have. Callaghan was able to work his way in. He's got a certain charm, you know: Uncle Jim. He used that very often.

Personal History

Mother's Side

My father met my mother in Spitalfields. Her family was by comparison well off. She had a number of brothers, all working as diamond-cutters. My maternal grandparents, whom I remember well, were a striking couple. My grandfather was small, but of tough physique. When, as a result of an accident, he died at the age of ninety-three, he was still fit.

My grandmother was a tall, beautiful woman with the character and serenity of her |Dutch| ancestors. She ruled her family with a rod of iron.

My parents' marriage was a love match. Until my birth they lived in my grandparents' house. Soon after my father had found rooms, he fell out of work, the reason being his protest about labour conditions. Conditions were very tough in those first years for my parents . . . a contributory factor in my father's interest in trade unionism.

In this period of depression, my father was forced to leave London to seek work in the provinces: Nottingham, Leicester, and then to Newcastle where he had relations. He obtained funds and started a seamen's outfitters in South Shields. Only rarely could he send my mother any money: she was fortunate in getting a job as cook in an institution for poor children. An early memory I have is of accompanying her. It was winter, and quite dark, as she served platters of porridge to hundreds of hungry youngsters in a gas-lit hall. There were many charitable organizations . . . It is not intended as criticism of the good they did to say that contributions for their work mostly came from people who thus achieved the twin results of easing their consciences and lessening the risks of social upheaval. There was strong belief that poverty was a sin. The sinners were legion. I have ugly memories of crowds squabbling for bread distributed by these charities.

Although my father could not support his family, he sent for me. I can still recall when my mother took me to Liverpool Street station and put me in charge of a guard on the Great Northern Line. I was only seven years old.

Sir Winston Churchill

When I got back [to the House of Commons in 1935] I listened, I wanted to listen, to the speeches of Churchill warning the country — how right he was — with Nancy [Lady] Astor sitting behind him, almost spitting at him. Or walking through the lobby, with only Brendan Bracken, Bob Boothby or Anthony Eden.

J.D. "Did you think him right, at the time — not with hindsight?"
I've taken much interest in defence over the years. I would think I was more influenced by Winston Churchill and those speeches than by anything else. War – I didn't like the idea. But somehow I felt this man must be doing the right thing.

What also influenced me was the way he was being treated by the Tories. I often thought about Churchill's reactionary attitudes to the working class, the Labour Party, Socialism, and so on — but he somehow stirred up my patriotic sentiments which I had from way back in the Boer War, seeing the volunteers going off to South Africa, waving Union Jacks.

A Lasting Friendship

Churchill asked me to accept a position [*during the war, which Manny declined.*] I said, 'We [the Opposition] won't embarrass you. We want to win.' He said, 'I know.' That's why we remained friends.

[Later] Churchill said, 'I always wanted you in my government.' He used to say the same to my first wife, who became very friendly with him.

* * *

Churchill said things about me that surprised the House. When Anthony Head was Minister of Defence — long after me — he was talking away after I had been speaking in the debate. Anthony referred to me, and as he was doing so, Churchill pulled his coat and made him sit down. Anthony must have wondered what it was — and so did the House. Then Churchill made a short speech — his speeches were usually read but this was impromput — and he spoke of me, and my work at Defence, what I'd done for the country . . . amazing, embarrassing almost. Churchill was so effusive and complimentary about my work as Minister of Defence. After he'd said it, he sat down, and Anthony went on with his speech.

* * *

I can remember when a number of us were invited to Hyde Park Gate |Churchill's London House in Kensington| on, I think, his birthday | after he'd resigned|. There was Jo Grimond, representing the Liberals; Selwyn Lloyd, who I think was Speaker at the time, and Harold Wilson, and Cox, Clerk to the House, and myself. We stood behind Churchill, who was sitting in a chair. In the photo in *The Times* I'm standing next to the chair and he's talking to me. He didn't seem to know any of the others. He wouldn't have known Wilson.

I was the only one he really knew, because I used to chivvy him in the House. I recall he called for an attendant and asked for a glass of champagne, and gave me one. He called for another one, and a box of cigars. He handed me one and I put it in my pocket. He said, 'You light it!' I thought, there's a crowd outside and I can't come out of Churchill's house smoking a cigar — could be the end of me! He really was remarkably friendly, and particularly in front of the others.

* * *

Of Sir Winston Churchill's grandson, Winston Churchill, MP.: We agree on only one subject — Defence.

Coal

Naturally, Manny often returned to the question of the coal industry. Perhaps his opinion of its current status was best summarized in this statement of lost opportunity:

Surely the proper thing to have done |when coal was nationalized| is what I recommended to Clem Attlee: to integrate the fuel and power industries. To process coal, to produce anything from coal you can — almost anything. We could have done it. Shilly-shallying, spending money in small bits: No good.

Partnership Rejected

They were debating in the Lords |1981| on a submission by the EEC about consultation with employees. Our |Labour's| principal speaker was Professor McCarthy, one of the leading authorities on trade unions.

He knows his stuff, but he waves his arms about when speaking; can't stand him. He's talking about the need for consultation. That's a thing that can't be done because people won't participate. It never occurred to him to look up the records, when he would have found that when I was nationalizing the mines, preparing the legislation, and I met the miners' leaders — every one of them now dead — and they came to me and asked for certain reforms, I said, 'You can only have these reforms when we've appointed the Coal Board.' And I said, 'What I want you to do is select a few of your number, an elite, as designate members of the Coal Board. And I want you to regard yourselves not as employees but as partners in the industry — not only for the purposes of wages and safety, but for administration and organization.'

Do you know what they did? William Lawther replied, 'No, we're not interested in that. What we want is the promise of a five-day week.'

I said, 'Appoint three of your members to be designate members. What you need to discuss is the kind of organization you want established.' What could you have better, more important, than that? For other industries as well.

J.D. "Did any miners' leaders go on the Board?"
The answer is, I offered two [places] eventually — one to Edwards, the miners' past president, and the other to Arthur Horner, who was a communist, by the way. What do you think happened? Edwards couldn't take it alone. Horner consulted Harry Pollitt, communist leader, and came back to me — he was easily the most impressive member of the delegation though a communist — he came back to me and said, 'Sorry, I'd like to be [on the Board] but Harry says, "No, you're not to take part in administration: your job is to protect the interest of your members".'

That's history. What has been done with that document?*

What they [the miners] demanded was — either you give us this or that or you won't get the coal. Could I have revealed that to the public? Could I have got up in the House of Commons and said the miners' leaders said that unless I give them the five-day week and extra wages and rations [*stringent food rationing persisted*] and all the rest, I don't

---

To repeat Manny's query: What has been done with that document?

I was writing my *Conflict Without Malice* (Odhams, 1955), and I wanted to get the documents. There were two conferences, in '46 and '47, during which we discussed the demand for reforms . . . For thirty years I kept quiet [about the miners' ultimata and rejection of partnership]. What happens? I asked the Ministry of Fuel and Power if I could have a copy. They declined on the grounds it was an official secret. So I did the book out of my memory.

get the coal. Should I have got up and said that? Do you think I was daft? Could I have got up and said we'd got 80 per cent absenteeism in my own constituency amongst the miners? So I kept quiet.

The miners were offered a partnership. Imagine if they'd accepted it! What would have happened in the industry? It would have been a different industry altogether.

Technological Possibilities

I ventured to say this in the House of Lords not long ago: I'm in favour of helping the miners. But I said to the Lords, 'Be careful. In America they don't go and dig down for coal. It's there on the surface. In Australia the same — all over the world — that's where you get coal now. You don't have to go down digging for it as we do, and under the sea off the Durham coast — miles under the sea with all the costs involved. We don't need to do that. We're out of date, outmoded. Of course we've got plenty of coal. It's our only [virtually inexhaustible] source of energy — but not properly used.

God knows, I did try to put that right when I was in government. But there you are — and one of these days what are we going to find? Pits will close — and they're going to spend millions of pounds on new coalfields.

J.D. "I remember, during the war, speaking with a colliery manager in South Wales, who propounded the idea — new to me — that coal should be left in the ground and burnt there to tap its energy . . ."
They have experimented in Lancashire. It requires, of course, first of all the consent of the miners, who don't like the idea of it. But it would also lead to a great deal of additional expenditure and we don't know if it would work very well.

What I would like to see, what I tried myself when I was Secretary for Mines — I wanted to produce more oil from coal — benzine, tars, all sorts of things — everything from coal, which of course we can do. It meant expenditure, but when I think of what has been spent by the National Coal Board, new machinery and all the rest for increased production — apart from very high wages — when I think of that, the whole set-up of the National Coal Board . . .! If we had spent much of the money on coal PROCESSING, I think we would have produced a form of energy much more successful than anything we ended up with.

J.D. "South Africa manages to produce, in an emergency, as much oil as she needs from coal."
It was started here by Lloyd George in the First World War, with a pilot scheme in the old Metropolitan Gas Works. When I became Secretary

for Mines in 1924 I got to know all about this. I had a scientific reasearch man in my department and we agreed we would revive the pilot scheme; at the end of the war it had gone. But I needed money. I understood I needed at least £30,000 to revive it. I went to see [Philip] Snowden, who was Chancellor of the Exchequer, who was very friendly and partial to younger members of the party. I got £30,000 from him and revived the scheme. A year later I was out.

J.D. "The idea had been to extract oil?"
Yes. And when I became Secretary for Mines again [1929], I managed to get details of a whole series of projects — from Germany and other places — but they were so expensive it was impossible to put them into operation. I couldn't get the government to find the money for them.

When I was asked by Attlee to leave Mines and go to the War Office, I said, 'I don't want to go. I'm all right in what I'm doing — never mind about the Coal Board "crisis" and all that.' Of course he agreed, because there was no "crisis". He said, 'What do you want to do?' And I said, 'I want to integrate the three coal and power industries — gas, electricity, oil — over which I had control at the time — and these I want to build up into a single energy industry.' His answer was, 'No. I haven't got time for matters like that.' I went to the War Office.

If I'd been there [at Mines], I'd really have made a job of that [integrated energy industry]. I'd have forced it through. When I think of the chances we've missed, either by being lazy, or unconcerned, or haven't had enough money — or because of self-interest or because of jealousy — you didn't want another Minister doing better than yourself — that sort of thing . . .

What a shambles it's been, what a shambles!

Constitutional Matters

J.D. "There's been a lot of talk about whether we should have a written Constitution — or a Bill of Rights."
I've heard the discussion. Lord Hailsham has often referred to it in speeches — remarkable speeches, highly intelligent observations on the Constitution and other questions. But I don't believe we gain very much by using language in order to govern or administer.

We accept certain principles in this country. We accept the freedom to express ourselves. We accept the right to call upon those responsible for law and order to protect the citizen. We have these rights. I've had all the rights I've ever wanted. I can't remember any particular right I was refused.

[*I put some arguments advanced for a formal Constitution*]

If you effect changes of this character in the Constitution, by inserting words instead of accepting principles, do you solve any problems? When you're faced with poverty, or considerable unemployment, a decline in trade, do you solve any of these problems by inserting words into a Constitution, which could be interpreted in various ways and cause complicated and expensive litigation? Is it worth while, if things are going on fairly well?

It's not a written Constitution we want, it's just a bit of common sense.

Crime and Punishment

There is far more violence than there was in the old days. There was some violence then but nothing like the terrorism to which we have been subjected in recent years. Murder — far more than occurred before. What are we to do about this?

It is natural and inevitable that the more we hear of some violent act, some act of cruelty, that we should become angry, seek retaliation. Something must be done. The culprit concerned should be sent to prison, should be detained for many years. And some people go further. When capital punishment was in operation [it was on the basis of], 'We can't be bothered with people like that in our community.'

J.D. "Were you an abolitionist?"

I supported Sydney Silverman, when thirty or so years ago he introduced a Bill into the House of Commons for the abolition of capital punishment. I was one of seven sponsors of the Bill. But I must say I've been inclined from time to time to change my mind when some act of atrocity has occurred, for which there seemed no civilized reason. On the other hand, I would often ask myself, 'WHY did it happen?' One oscillates, finds it difficult to come to a conclusion.

J.D. "The public has clearly demonstrated as being in favour of bringing back some form of death penalty. Would you support a Bill which brought in capital punishment in cases of terrorism, killing police officers during commission of a crime — certain of those sorts of category?"

Well, here again I oscillate. I have feelings of fury, inclination to advise extreme action against the cuprit. Sympathy for the victim is not enough. But, inevitably, I allow my mind to ramble over the subject. Why did it happen? Take the situation in Northern Ireland . . .

J.D. "We're talking of crime unrelated to politics."

I agree that is different: we can deal with that in another context. In ordinary cases, one reads of someone committing a crime which has caused wounds, death, and one wants to take retaliatory action. I offer a thought: we ought to bring back capital punishment, but not in every case. It must depend on the nature of the crime. I would take all that into account. I feel there are some people involved in criminal acts who are not proper persons to retain in our community. We're better off without them. Therefore, the only thing is to re-introduce capital punishment. Yet, when I say that, I've always got in mind some cases that occurred in the past, in my experience, where innocent people have been found guilty and sentenced to death — and [sometimes] executed. There's the case of Oscar Slater. I lived quite near to where the event occurred, the West End of Glasgow — anything but 'West End'! I was married, with two children. Just across the street was the road where the murder occurred. An old woman was killed, and articles of hers stolen. A man [Oscar Slater] was arrested. After a long trial, he was sentenced to death and imprisoned [on reprieve] at Peterhead in north Scotland. His case was taken up by quite a number of people: I was a bit involved as a Town Councillor so far as petitions were concerned. It was discovered by many of us that the prosecution had introduced his general character. He was a gambler. He was responsible for prostitution and that sort of thing and had a really bad reputation. He was a foreigner — also Jewish I believe. He was in prison eighteen years before release. [*We recalled Conan Doyle's efforts.*] He had actually been prosecuted and sentenced not for murdering someone, but because he was a rascal.

J.D. "I don't think anyone would favour introducing capital punishment across the board. A man robbing a bank, and shooting down in cold blood, before witnesses, a security officer — that is, murder for gain. Nothing can conceivably be said in favour of such a criminal."

There is always the feeling, 'I wonder why he did it.'

J.D. 'Do we mind WHY he went out with a gun to commit a crime?"

But why did he DO that? What caused him to do it? Is the man sane?

Was he starving? [*Starvation is certainly an original excuse for murder today, but I did not make the point.*] All these considerations are in one's mind. Although I do agree that in cases in which there can be no doubt at all, that person ought to be sentenced to death.

J.D. "The House of Commons has consistently refused to reintroduce even very limited capital punishment — against clear public demand."
It was almost agreed when I was in government on more than one occasion that where there was a murderous act against a member of the police force, capital punishment should pertain. But they always hesitated, towards the end, on the question of whether it was a deterrent. That's always been the principal factor. If society insists on revenge, retaliation for a criminal act, and resorts to capital punishment, whether it deters people from acting in a similar fashion . . . statistics don't prove that it is so.

Transportation Renewed
The prison crisis — of course it's not new. The situation has become more serious — prison governors criticizing — at their wits' ends to administer prison life . . . What's to be done bothers me a bit. More prisons available in '85 — use of unemployed as temporary warders — some talk of an amnesty. Ridiculous. Some have talked about certain prisoners being 'political' and being allowed to go out when they please and have the weekend off — but you can't have that. And there are others who say judges should cut sentences . . . that's been said over and over again and repeated in Parliament — though not in the Lords . . . it is countered by horrible crimes by young people, mostly psychopaths. What is to happen to psychopaths? Are they going to be detained, as some have been sentenced, for life — twenty, thirty years' detention at the expense of the public, occupying accommodation, using foodstuffs?

J.D. "You're making a case for capital punishment."
Manny repeated his ambivalent attitude to that question.

J.D. "Let me put a notion to you, a far-out one. With hardened criminals, serving ten years or more, if one was to take a place like St Kilda — no longer populated but which we know can support people — and establish a form of penal colony there. They could tend sheep, lead a reasonably normal life — almost impossible to escape — warders rotated and highly recompensed . . ."
It's an excellent idea — advocated some time ago — but an expensive operation.

29

J.D. "Would it be more expensive than keeping them in prison?"
You've got to get the island.

J.D. "St. Kilda was evacuated before the war."
There'd be opposition from those nearby.

J.D. "There's nobody near St Kilda — for some hundred miles."
It's a point worth considering. But, again, there's something about it one dislikes. If I had to choose between capital punishment for the hardened criminal, the psychopath, and an island where he would be detained for several years — perhaps for ever — I'd prefer capital punishment.

J.D. "Some of the people whom I would submit as being suitable for transportation would not have committed murders, and by no means would all murderers attract a transportation sentence. Those transported would have committed hideous crimes and be a menace to society. One would be taking worthless people out of the community. And the deterrent would be terrific."

Personal History

Simple Pleasures

Life was not altogether drab in those days of childhood. When we were living in London, in Petticoat Lane I could get a dish of hot peas for a farthing (0.125p), and liver and mashed potatoes for a penny (0.5p). Eggs were 36 for a shilling (5p) — or more cheap when competition was keen.

When my father was in work he liked to enjoy himself. I can recall him singing some of the old-time ditties: Irish comedians were then the vogue. My mother also liked to sing. She preferred Irish love songs. Those carefree times occurred when work was available, and food and rent money no longer scarce.

Fortunately, though my father read very little apart from subjects which were his immediate interest, my mother was a great lover of books. She read all kinds of novel, probably her escape from too frequent child-bearing and far too frequent bouts of poverty. So what she read, I read. Perhaps that is why my interest is so easily aroused by stories of adventure and heroism.

Civilized Society

My concern is not about that aspect, though I agree it's important — very important indeed. My concern relates to my objective of a civilized community. The more I read about these hardened, these mad criminals, psychopaths ... my principal objective, as a politician, as a citizen of the world, is to create civilized communities ...

I see no prospect of my ideal of a civilized country coming into existence during my lifetime. And that is a very serious thing. One is inclined to lose interest in public affairs. One feels one wants to wash one's hands of the whole business: 'If that's the way you're going to carry on, I'll live my own life and not bother about it at all.'

J.D. "You can't have a civilized community, which I think most people would subscribe to as an ideal, unless you remove from it uncivilized elements, human or otherwise."
I don't know what you mean by 'remove them'. Dispose of them?

J.D. "I don't necessarily mean dispose of them; perhaps by the transportation to which we've just referred or by capital punishment in some cases — not in all cases, because that would be uncivilized itself."
It's a bleak prospect. So far as one can see, over the years there are to be people in prison, sentenced to imprisonment for [most of their lives]. It's a terrible prospect. And there is the danger of yielding to the 'compassionate' people, the people who aver that people ought not to be imprisoned at all, that they ought to be 'educated' to become civilized. The problem is much more serious even than I have made out. There's so much criminality — particularly in the young. What about our education? What about our churches ...?

J.D. "There's a moral breakdown ... there's a breakdown in discipline. A young person knows that even if he commits a fairly serious crime, nothing much is going to happen to him. If they knew they were going to get some pretty nasty punishment they might think twice. But they see people getting away with a two-year suspended sentence or being meaninglessly fined. There's no further 'going to the Moor' for penal servitude. Criminals really didn't like that at all. I've known some of them."
That advocates longer sentences, and that's the thing that worries me. You've got a chap of twenty, sentenced to life — thirty years. When he comes out, he's no longer sane. That's wrong. But I come back to the point: isn't it a terrible reflection on society, on its leaders, the Church, the politicians, the Press, and now TV ... instead of the situation improving because of education — it's had very little effect ...

J.D. "Increased criminality — not only in this country — has gone hand in hand with material improvement. Even the Swiss . . ."
That's one view — people want more. If we diagnose the complaint, I would say one of the main causes is the increasing population — all over the world — the cramming together of millions of people, often in accommodation that's highly unsatisfactory. Also, lack of interest by the teaching profession. Is our educational system at fault? I'd say it is.

J.D. "The quality of teaching is so poor — declining. We know what Shaw said — 'Those who can, do. Those who can't, teach.'"
We can't just stand aside and let things go on without doing something about it.

Defence

When I became Minister of Defence [1950–1] I decided on a rearmament programme, as a result of which I lost my seat on the national executive [of the Labour Party] because there were so many against me. I was determined to go ahead — because I believed in it. I decided that the length of service of the National Serviceman should be two years.

J.D. "The regular forces are much against it — but would you think there is anything to be said for reintroducing conscription?"
I waver a bit on this because of my knowledge of the subject. I could come outright for conscription because we need the manpower. I could come out for it because we might find ourselves in the position of suddenly having to decide on it as we did in 1916.

The Territorials
If we decided on conscription, a man's got to be trained. It requires sometimes three or four Regulars to train one man. It's a very expensive business. I would rather do it this way: by building up a Territorial force. [*A small increase in the Territorials was decided on in 1984.*]
I've said it so often, I still go on saying it — I've attacked many Defence Ministers: how many men have you got? What is the target? I'd ask. I know that if you've got a vast number of men with some idea how to use a rifle, how to shoot at a target, some men who can endure for a time the sort of anguish that's associated with warfare — thinking of your family and all that — THAT makes all the difference. I don't believe it's possible for us to avoid defeat without a vast number of Territorials. We have been building them up, but I've never been satisfied with their training.

When I was Minister of Defence, I decided we must do something about the Territorials. I suggested to the Director of Auxiliary Forces — I forget his name — that we must have a campaign in support of the Territorials. He didn't think much of it. He thought he was doing very well — as they all do. You put someone in a position: he thinks he's doing well. He doesn't want interference, particularly from a politician. But this man was dealing with someone he didn't understand.

I said, 'Look here — I want you to organize a march through the City of London, with the Lord Mayor taking the salute. In particular, I want you to get two Highland regiments.' He didn't think it would be possible, but, 'I'll consider it, sir'.

He came back a couple of weeks later and said it was impossible, particularly to get the Highland regiments. Know what I did? I said, 'Go and do it.' I insisted. As a result — I can see it now — the Lord Mayor in his robes, and the troops marching through the City. Why did I do it? Because I thought it was the correct thing to do. And it couldn't affect the Regulars to any extent. The Territorials could train themselves — given the chance, with the right people superintending operations. Much more of that's got to be done. There's got to be proper training. You've got to have the proper men at the top. Very often there's a General who doesn't believe in that sort of thing: he's a Regular himself and contemptuous of this sort of thing. In fact, we never could have succeeded in any [modern] war without the Territorials. Again, as in the political field, in the military field it's the myths that trouble us. The myth that you can have a trip-wire effect in Europe to keep the Russians out. With a vast air-power, you think they won't send a ballistic missile, a theatre one, a small one but enough to shatter a thousand people? They'll use everything they've got, and we've got to be prepared for that.

Unilateral Disarmament

You might say, why not stop it in some way. Now the unilateral attitude won't stop anything — only convince the Russians they can get away with it.

How are we going to stop it? I would do as I've already suggested. If the Russians are having trouble in Poland, or Romania, if our Intelligence services have any knowledge of clandestine movements operating, if we're getting information — then we offer quite frankly to negotiate. Not the way it's being done, but in a surreptitious, back-room sort of way. Let Mrs Thatcher or President Reagan say, 'Look, we'd like to sit down with you as soon as possible and discuss every aspect of the problem.'

When everything is going right for the Russians, you can't do anything. But they're having trouble in Afghanistan, in Poland, food problems — and they're building up huge forces that have got to be maintained: if you've got three or four million men constantly in the Forces, you've got to feed them . . . Now's the time for Reagan to say, 'Now's the time, Mr President, for you and I to get to table.' A great deal depends on how you tackle a problem. You can do it in a [normal] diplomatic fashion; on the whole I don't prefer that.

Getting On With Generals

If you yourself know what's wanted, and you're firm about it, people will follow you. I remember one occasion when I was misled by some statistics, and I called a meeting of the Army Council. It was wintertime, and there were about five or six of us gathered round the fire while I talked. I was speaking about manpower. I said, 'Only last week I was talking to General so-and-so and he told me that a certain number of men were required for a particular task, and I accepted it. Now you're giving me figures that are quite different. What am I going to do?' Then I said, 'Make up your bloody minds what you want!' There were high people there, like [Field Marshals] Slim and Templer. And I said, 'Make up your bloody minds, why can't you?'

J.D. "And did they?"
They did! I believe that made me more popular — I was undoubtedly a success; that's generally known — more popular than anything else I could have done. They understood my language: I was one of them. The idea that I was top man didn't bother me . . . The people I had to work with in the War Office and the Ministry of Defence — the military people, were the best people I ever co-operated with. I must say that. They may have been kidding me — I don't know — but I'm not as innocent as all that! When I compare [my experience at War Office and Defence] with the Ministry of Fuel and Power, what a contrast! you'd think they were in different worlds.

J.D. "On the question of generals — Lord Carver?"
I have a problem there. I don't like Carver. I think Carver thinks too much of himself. He ought never to have been made Field-Marshal. He's taken the line which is acceptable to many military people that you must rely on the conventional and give up the idea of the nuclear altogether. He's contemptuous of any naval build-up. But the man who sits in front of him, and behind me, in the Lords is the man whom I admire more than anyone else in the military sphere — Admiral of the Fleet Lord Hill-Norton, who is, of course, very angry they're reducing the naval forces. And he's right, because if you can't protect your shipping, you're

going to starve. He's absolutely right about that. But I think it would be difficult to talk with Carver . . . You sometimes get that impression of people — you don't want to approach them.

. . . Field Marshal Lord Harding — that's the man I worked with: he called himself an employee of mine. He must have been very good to have been made a Field Marshal: he had experience in two wars.

If you're in political life you occasionally find yourself not altogether disliking a person but careful about that person. Now Harding I like, as I liked Slim. He had a temper, the rudest man I ever met, but I recognized his ability.

[*I recounted a brush I had with (the then Lieut.-Colonel) Templar at Le Mans in early 1940.*]

Templar was one of the young generals when I was at the Ministry. When I picked him out myself as a possible Chief of General Staff, Monty didn't think much of him at the time — possibly because of his rudeness. He was a political soldier — knew his stuff. But there were so many others — wonderful people . . .

War I hate. But I recognize one's got to defend oneself. As I said to the Lords: 'Our prime consideration must be the defence of the UK. In that sense, we must use ALL our resources; including our allies, instead of fighting with them.'

CAN War Be Avoided?

How is one going to stop war? Isn't it a remarkable thing that there isn't a single country [of any consequence] in the world – however large, however small — that hasn't got Defence. Every one of them, small countries hardly worth talking about, has some measure of Defence. Why? The point is that it is a very natural desire to protect oneself.

I don't doubt for a moment the honesty and integrity of [unilateral disarmament] people. When [Lord] Soper was speaking in the Lords, I said I didn't doubt for a moment the noble Lord's integrity. We disagree.

J.D. "Is there a remote possibility that the so-called hawkish element in the Pentagon would seriously think of a pre-emptive strike against Russia?"

I haven't the least doubt there are people like that in the Services. It has been suggested in certain quarters — but that's only people talking silly stuff. I can understand that someone who has been serving for many years, but has no experience of war, might say, 'We've got the stuff . . .' and I've sometimes wondered whether the Americans haven't got some things about which we don't know anything at all — keeping them very quiet because it wouldn't be wise to talk about them. Don't forget the Israelis . . .

35

J.D. "In a small way, the Israelis have shown the value of the pre-emptive strike."

I think that would be nonsense. Unless you've got superiority, unless you've got something the others haven't yet, pre-emptive strikes are out of the question. Personally, I think it would be immoral to do it. And I think it would be undesirable because I don't think it would be effective. It would have to be tremendously devastating, and I don't think there can be any guarantee of that. Besides, in the end I doubt if you could defeat Russia, because of her vast resources.

Nuclear Defence Essential

Some [Labour politicians] say, 'Oh, no, we can't get out of NATO. However, we've got to get rid of nuclear weapons.' And what is left? Suppose we rely in future on unilateral, or even multilateral, disarmament — or whatever you like to call it — reducing expenditure on defence . . . conventional, relying on the Army, what we've got left of the Navy, and the Air Force . . . this against the might, the weapons, the manpower at the disposal of the Soviet Union! In three weeks' time they'd be in this country if we left it to conventional weapons. And they [defence critics] forget that even our land forces are armed with nuclear weapons — of only limited range, but nuclear. And the Navy, if there's anything left of it at all — unless we're going to abolish submarines and all the rest of it — is mostly nuclear.

The whole thing is so contradictory. I would be in favour of doing this . . . If we are not going to be allowed to have nuclear weapons, I don't want conventional ones either — because the conventional ones [on their own] are not going to be worth tuppence. In three weeks the Russians are here. What's going to prevent them? We don't have to have the Russians [themselves] going in. The East Germans could do the job. The East Germans would wash the West Germans out right away . . . Holland and Denmark don't matter very much . . . thousands of parachutists into this country — and no nuclear weapons at all. We put up the white flag — surrender.

That's what absence of nuclear defence means — and that is one thing the British public will NOT stand. Therefore, when it comes down to discussing armaments in detail, all this stuff [*Manny waves some Labour party (pro-*CND*) documents*] will have no effect whatsoever.

I'm a zealot as far as Defence is concerned: I won't yield an inch on them . . . We must have a nuclear deterrent.

See MONTGOMERY.

Personal History

Efforts At Independence

I went to school for a year in South Shields. The Seamen's out-fitters business of my father's was then nearing disaster. He decided to try Glasgow. He sent for my mother and sister and for nearly three years I had regular schooling. When I was eleven, my father moved to another part of Glasgow and he then employed me as an errand boy. My organized education was over. My melancholy reflections because of this I have spoken of and how I was consoled when years afterwards I saw in the House of Commons some of the products of universities and high scholastic institutions.

I became tired of running errands for my father. I got a job as message, later van-boy, with a tobacco firm. The pay was 5 shillings (25p) a week. My father then conceived the notion I should be trained as a tailor's cutter. It was no use: I had no gift for the job.

A variety of jobs followed. One was with a chair manufacturers at 6 shillings a week. Work started at 6 a.m. One rosy prospect came at the Singer sewing machine factory. A foreman promised me a job at the fabulous wage of 17 shillings: the 15-mile walk to and from the factory seemed well worth it. To get this job I had walked out of home one morning. Now came the realization I dared not return. I met some chums and they collected eightpence so I could get a bed for the night. Then my mother, who had been searching for me all day, came along. Home I went. I was back in the family tailoring business.

Democracy

Our democracy is poised on a very precarious part of the cliff.

J.D. "It could be argued by both marxists and some people of the Right right that democracy has failed."
Democracy meant over the years — from the Chartist movement, the Reform movement — to gain representation in Parliament. That wasn't democracy at all. You couldn't get real democracy until the majority of people in the country had expressed their view on a particular topic and seen to it that the government carried it out . . .

J.D. "It's only in recent times that democracy became a respectable word. Has not some of the rot in democracy set in with universal suffrage? At eighteen, any half-baked yob has the same vote as I have. Do you think the right to vote should be earned, by age or other qualifications?"
What do we mean by democracy? We mean the working people wanting more power. There's no longer any democracy amongst local authorities: the government tells them to do this and that, and if they don't they won't get grants.

Democracy has never really existed. Take Russia — there's no democracy there. It isn't a dictatorship of the proletariat. What is there? A tyranny.

J.D. "The one country that gets nearest to political democracy must be Switzerland with its semi-independent cantons and any national issue decided by referenda. And it seems to work."
That democracy is inhibited by finance. Who are the bosses there? The Swiss banks.

J.D. 'It suits the Swiss to have it that way."
Who benefits?

J.D. "The standard of living . . ."
Manny was dismissive, but then:
It's a [cantonal] system I'd advocate for this country.* I was talking with some of my colleagues and I said we must get back[?] to a regional system. But, of course, Switzerland is a very small country.

See GOVERNMENT.

Drinking

Our conversations were judiciously lubricated. Manny poured generously:

J.D. "You've got a nice heavy hand I must say. I think you learned to pour Scotch in Scotland, where a wee dram means a fairly hefty tot. I bet you didn't drink Scotch before you went up to Glasgow — don't suppose you drank much there, in your early days; wouldn't have been able to afford it even at three shillings a bottle."

Do you know, the whole time I lived in Glasgow I never tasted whisky. Not until 1923. I went to Parliament in 1922. In 1923 I decided to move from Glasgow to London. All that time I never drank whisky. My father did. He'd offer it to me and laugh when I refused. I never drank liquor of any kind until several years after I was in Parliament. In fact, I don't believe I touched it until I began to attend lunches when I became a Minister.

J.D. "But when you were in Scotland you'd have been moving around where a lot of drinking was going on."

Drunkenness: I've witnessed it. It was shocking . . . I never drank. I'm sure the reason was that Keir Hardie, the founder of the Indpendent Labour Party, had been a Temperance reformer and remained an abstainer till he died. Those of us who were members of the ILP followed him.

When I started attending lunches, it was wine. I found it was producing gout. So I had to give that up. For forty to fifty years I've drunk whisky. I never drink wine at all.

J.D. "On the subject of drink — there's a tremendous amount of drinking goes on in the House of Commons. It is often referred to. Or is it some sort of rumour?"

You've got to remember it can be a very monotonous job — long hours. I've often seen members spifflicated — even seen Cabinet Ministers that way.

I hardly ever go into the bar [in the House of Lords]. I sometimes go into the Guest Room if I have a visitor. Sometimes I feel the need for a tot of whisky. So I've got a locker, in one of the corridors. So I've got a key and I open it and I take the bottle and do that – [*Manny makes a pouring motion*] — and if someone is passing I say, 'Just taking my medicine — every four hours.' But I don't offer them any!

* * *

As CIGS, Monty [Field Marshal Montgomery] came into my room. He never went through the secretaries' room: he came in through the side door. There's a story that with previous Secretaries of War, when Monty came into the room, they stood up. The idea of me standing up for anyone was too much! He comes in and says, 'Hullo' I says, 'Hullo.' He comes over to my desk and he has something behind his back — a bottle of whisky. I say, 'What's this?' 'It's for you. It's my allocation from the NAAFI,' he says.

I was doing a BBC programme, and in the course of it I told that story and I mentioned it was Black & White. Now you're not supposed to advertise on the BBC, but the Distillers people heard this, and I was in my room in the House of Commons when the attendant phoned and said, 'Minister, there's a parcel for you.' I said, 'Send it up.' It was a couple of bottles of Black & White with a note from Buchanan's. I phoned immediately and asked for the chairman and said, 'You mustn't do this. A Member of Parliament is not supposed to accept gifts. Why did you do this?' They said, 'You gave us a wonderful advertisement — worth thousands to us.' So I said, 'What we'll do, in order to make things all right — have you ever been to the House of Commons? Come down and have lunch with me.' He asked if he could bring his vice-chairman. So they came down to the Annexe and had lunch. Cost me more than two bottles of whisky!

* * *

Now and again, Monty would come in in the same style and say, 'That's your medicine.' That's when I decided on what I call 'My medicine, every four hours.'

Then Monty went off to be an international soldier and I got [Field Marshal] Slim — a wonderful person — but he drank. So I didn't get any whisky. Do you know what I got from him? He'd put his hand in his pocket and pull a cigar out. He didn't smoke, but he said, 'Whenever I go to lunch, I take a cigar for you.'

Education

J.D. 'Private education: some members of the Labour Party have suggested it should be forbidden by law."
There are two aspects to this. Should children be educated on the basis of the power of the purse? Should the best educational facilities be provided for them simply because the parents can afford to pay for them? The other side is this: should any children, possibly with potential ability, he prevented from enjoying the best facilities simply because the parents can't afford it? I've got no strong feelings about it. [*Manny explained that after losing his Parliamentary seat in 1931, he could not send his two elder children to university.*] If I could have afforded it, I would have sent them. Why? Because I would have liked them to have the education I failed to obtain. My grandchildren — one is managing director of Mobil Oil's engineering department in Florida; my granddaughter has been in France working with the British Council. Both with degrees. My son sent them to Mill Hill School — could well afford it. What's wrong with that? The other children: they've had the best education we could afford.

On the other hand, I don't like a system where a child has potential and yet is not able to use it. Therefore, I accept both systems. The comprehensive school with the highest possible standards available – and that's got to be understood — and where [a child] shows exceptional ability send him to another [private] school. If children are sent to Eton or Winchester — quite frankly, it doesn't bother me in the least. That's one of the subjects on which I disagree with the Labour Party.

Take my own case. I had practically no education — and I've been troubled about it. What might have happened if I'd had a decent education? Why was I deprived of that? It doesn't bother me in the least.

J.D. 'The chances are that had you had a formal education, you wouldn't be anything like as well educated as you are. You wouldn't have had the incentive to read and study and go to the public library."
Put it another way [*Manny laughs heartily*]. I'd never have become a Cabinet Minister! I would never have been Minister for Defence — never nationalized the mines!

Looking back, I venture to say this: the fact that I had such a struggle was the best thing that could have happened to me. At the same time, I wonder if it wouldn't have been better if I'd had an education. Why? Because it would have been easier then to understand what I'm reading, instead of having to grapple with it. You'd be surprised how much knowledge I'd have liked to have had. I'm so curious and inquisitive about things — astronomy, philosophy, architecture — I don't know enough about them, and it annoys me.

* * *

At the moment, I'm reading over and over again *Hundred Best English Essays*.* Some are very difficult to fathom, Carlyle in particular. I get a paragraph, as I did with [T.H.] Huxley the other night, and I read it over and over and said, 'I must get the meaning of this. What does he mean by this?' And then I think, 'What am I doing this for? I can't take it with me.'

The tape at this juncture records glasses being replenished. J.D. opines that if an author cannot make his points clear, even on a second reading, then he has failed. It is evident Manny does not agree, though is too polite to suggest his companion suffers from intellectual indolence.

Education Should Be General Education

A knowledge of past events is essential because history relates to the future. Whatever happens in the future is conditioned to a considerable extent by what happened in the past. [At the same time] let us not place an excessive emphasis on historical events.

Now, in the sphere of education, if you cut down on education – and in particular on general education — I am not thinking of technical education — general education; that is to say an element of the arts, English, languages, relations with other countries — subjects which are essential to produce the civilized society one wants . . . *the sentence trailed off though its implication was clear.*

J.D. "It has been argued we are producing too many graduates who are educated beyond their powers to absorb that education."

If you are going to solve world problems, leaving aside the technological advance which is envisaged, which already has emerged, what is most essential is general education — that people should be better informed, capable of understanding events which are incomprehensible to people who haven't got the expertise. For unless you've got an educated community — not just on any specific topic but of a general character — then it's impossible to produce the kind of society it's the ambition of government and the electorate in general [to produce].

J.D. "Not everybody wants to be educated, do they?"

There's another aspect. If you're going to have the sort of education you

*Hundred Best English Essays, Earl of Birkenhead, Cassell, London, 1929.

get at Eton — Latin and Greek and that sort of thing is all very well — but we want something more than that. We want the sort of education so people are better informed — that when an MP is talking to them, they can understand what he says because they're as well informed as he is. There's nothing to prevent that if you've got the schools operating effectively, universities with the [necessary] finance. If you don't do that, and education is retarded to such an extent that in the next fifty years we find ourselves less civilized, less knowledgeable than at present, then any advantage we have through technological expertise will not help us. Technologists must be better informed on matters of general interest affecting the whole community, not just a section of it.

J.D. "Yet you can't educate people unless they wish to be educated. While a vast mass of people do, there are also millions who appear not to wish to be educated."
My answer would be that if you provide the facilities, people will take advantage of them.

J.D. "We have provided facilities, but there doesn't seem to be a higher degree of education as a result. We get boys and girls leaving school who can't do much more than write their own names. I don't think people become better informed by being educated. It comes back to self-education — such as yours. A lot of the more educated people have educated themselves — because they wanted to know more. The raising of the school-leaving age didn't improve the level of education one jot."
You are quite right in saying people must want to be educated. But I'm quite sure if you provide the facilities — as in my case. I took advantage of the facilities, having had a very limited [formal] education — practically none — when I was young. But the libraries were available, and the opportunity to express oneself. If that is infringed upon in any way, then education is retarded.

This particular conversation has been considerably abridged. I tried, vainly, to shake Manny's rather Utopian view of a widespread desire for education, simply because he himself yearned for it.

Personal History

The Young Patriot

The [family] shop was in the East End of Glasgow. Customers included Irishmen from North and South. In a workroom at the back of the shop customers and friends would cram long after working hours, talking and consuming beer and whisky which I had to bring from the pub.

My father sat on the fence on Irish topics, with the result both Southern Irish and Ulstermen respected and liked him. The fact that none of them ordered more than one cheap suit during scores of visits and time-wasting arguments did not affect him. The place was more like a club, with consequent effects on profits. Often customers would be out of work and they borrowed money from my father: they always paid it back. I suspected he borrowed from them during his own bad patches. One customer found he could not afford to take his best suit out of pawn on Saturday. So on the Sunday he would lean out of his tenement window wearing a boiled shirt with his moleskin working trousers. He kept up appearances.

By the time I was fourteen, the Boer question banished Home Rule [for Ireland] as the chief source of discussion. It broke out a day or two before my fifteenth birthday. I was a fervid Tory, ready to go to Africa and fight Kruger with my bare hands. Considering the war was bitterly opposed by all Socialists, it is not surprising my father banished me from the workroom at this period except on business.

I made up my mind to join the Navy. I looked older than I was, [but] when the officer learned my age, he told me to bring my parents' written consent. The result was the worst row of my life. Not long afterwards my father got me a job with a friend, also in tailoring. I still hated the work, but at least I got paid. My father had queer ideas about wages for one of the family.

Employment

What does it really matter? We're able to keep the unemployed, prevent them from starving — I wouldn't put it higher than that — they don't get a great deal and it's a burden on the taxpayers and on the Insurance Fund.

We accept all that. Does it really matter? Because at the end of the day we've got no assurance we'll be able to find employment for everybody. We may find at the end of the day that the recession has vanished and we've made the recovery that's being talked about . . . when that happy event occurs, there'll still be one and a half million people without work.

And what are we going to do? Then are they going to shorten the hours of labour from 39–40 to 30 or even to 20 [per week]? Are they going to do that? Are we going to provide the facilities for recreation and leisure to make life worth living? Or are we going to force people to leave the UK — to go to some of the areas in Brazil, and elsewhere, which yet have to be explored and exploited? Something of the sort will have to happen. Or they may discover other planets to which to transfer!

Or you may be faced with a problem — probably an inevitable problem — that you cannot find work for vast numbers, and people will retire at forty.

J.D. "We then come to another problem in that event — that you get a small labour force, albeit highly paid, supporting an enormous number of pensioners. And that workforce is going to say, 'We're getting fed up with this.'"

I think we're reaching that stage. And, of course, in politics you recognize that it's a serious problem. I reckon that already in this country we have 10 to 11 million pensioners. What's going to happen in the next few years when you get — what? — 20 million pensioners? And the rest of the country's got to keep them. But then, this has got to be taken into account: as years go by and our health and medical services ensure that people live longer, people who now retire at sixty may be working at the age of eighty. After all's said and done, if it's possible for me . . . if I can remain fairly active — even think about problems — if I'm able to take an interest in what's around me, if I can do that, many at the age of ninety will be able to do it. So we may find ourselves, because of longevity in the next twenty-five or fifty years, with numbers of people — vast numbers — living a full century and able to engage in activities either mental or physical. Now that could possibly happen. And that, alongside the reduction in hours of labour, will have solved the unemployment problem.

45

J.D. "But surely that does NOT *solve the unemployment problem. It makes it more acute. There'll be more people who, although hale and hearty and able to do all sorts of things, will have retired [say] at forty-five, and they've got to be supported. While they'll be active — reading, doing good works, even politics — they won't be producing anything. So the tiny labour force — 5 million? — will be supporting the fifty million pensioners."*

All we can do is give them a vote of thanks!

J.D. "The workers will say, 'We're not going to do it' — support the pensioners. They'll be out-voted by the pensioners but they — the 'worker bees' — will say there are too many drones."

I don't think we gain very much by suggesting we're going to have a vast array of problems. What I'm fully convinced about is we're going to see vast changes, if not within the next fifty years, certainly within the next century . . .

One would rather live in a world of change than one that's stagnant.

* * *

Production Not Enough

Manny had said Labour could no more solve unemployment than the Tories.

They [Labour politicians] talk about more investment: what are they going to do with it? We can go on producing and producing — with all the electronic equipment at our command. Not as good as Japan or the US, but we've still got facilities. We can go on producing. We've got some of the best companies — Plessey, Ferranti, other companies, and GEC, as good as anything in the world.

But what's the good of talking about production if you can't SELL the goods . . . I wish I were more involved.

Quality Of Life — Better Now?

J.D. "We've talked about change in quality of life — but do you really think that the great mass of people today, for all their improvement materially, are happier now then they were when you were twenty years old?"

. . . [after several relative clauses] People are NOT happier now than when I was younger. Admittedly, when I was younger, and suffered from unemployment and financial difficulties from time to time, one could hardly be happy, contented. But somehow, despite the struggle . . . of life as it was then, one got through without being surrounded by innumerable problems.

Manny warmed to his theme and became somewhat oratorical and

46

loquacious, discursive and digressive. Here was one of several instances where to listen to him was pleasant, but a transcription of the conversation is boring. To condense:

We have problems everywhere. There isn't a part of the world that isn't seething with troubles . . . You pick up a paper and on every page there are problems . . . the promiscuity — what one reads in the newspapers, hears about . . . the 'carrying on . . .' the goings-on of people in high places. Even if one doesn't probe into these matters, finds them distasteful, one knows they exist. When one was younger, one didn't seem to be troubled by them. The world itself seemed to be a better place, a happier place. Although I've watched beggars, dressed in the most clownish clothing, delving into dustbins for a crust of bread . . . if I'm to choose between the beggar and the unemployed man now reaching the age of sixty with no hope of getting a decent job in future — I think the beggar was happier. And those around him were happier.

One comes into public life full of hope and expectation, full of energy. And what for? To change the face of society, not to injure people, not to run people, but to help them. And we think we've solved a problem — only to create another. That is what is happening, and man in the world today, irrespective of where he is, he's unhappy and disturbed. It's a very sad business.

But perhaps we're too doleful, too pessimistic about it . . . but one has to face facts.

J.D. "The material life of people has improved immeasurably, and you — Socialists, the Labour Party — have played a very big part in improving the lot of even the unemployed man . . . Yet his actual quality of life, his relationships, are they as good as if he were unemployed on a pittance sixty years ago?"

. . . In the old days they were more contented. [Social Security] hasn't solved our problems.

J.D. "Isn't it true, the more you give people, the more they want?"

It happens in many cases. If people can get things without having to fight for them, they think it's easy — the State's a soft option. It's very difficult in public life. The task of the politician is more difficult than it ever was. If they're going to fulfil their promises, they're going to have to work harder than ever.

J.D. "From politicians, in opposition, I haven't yet seen any sensible suggestions that the man in the street can understand as to how unemployment can be solved. Grand oratory — but never any suggestions HOW . . ."

47

Nor did I get any suggestions How. Manny returned to dilating on the importance of Principles. We digressed to a discussion on a philosophical basis as to the possibility that war was "Nature's" way of controlling human populations now. Its old tools of famine and plague have largely been eradicated, and ought the NHS be diverted from pensioners in order to reduce the growing burden of their support? Broadly, Manny rejected the war theory and was amused by the notion of curtailing senior citizens' longevity, but, as in this rare instance he was more the listener than the talker, our exchanges are irrelevant.

A Moment of Pessimism

I'm sorry, I'm a bit pessimistic about things. Perhaps I wanted too much in my time. Perhaps, when I was younger, I had ideals, ambitions — not so much for myself as for the country as a whole, a country I came to love and for which I still have a strong affection and believe in — yes, still believe in — as good a country as any in the world and probably better than most . . . Things have not turned out as I hoped. It's very distressing, very depressing. You wonder how it's going to work out. And so I got to rely on my aspirations, the hope — I repeat myself — of a civilized community.

J.D. "It's a little bit Utopian, your hope for a civilized society, things being as they are."
I must say I'm inclined to agree. That's the worrying feature of it all. But there's a conflict of emotions — the things to which you aspire, and the FACTS of life. It's realities that matter.

The EEC

Manny said he had told the Labour Party: 'If some of the speeches that have been made [by leading party members] were made years ago, you'd have saved yourselves a heap of trouble. Many people who are now condemning the Common Market are the very people who insisted we must go in!' They were even going to expel me for my opposition to the Market.

J.D. "Is it practicable to withdraw?"
I must admit I am a bit ambivalent about it, for this reason. I was against going in, warned about it. They said, if we don't join, the country can never prosper; it we go in, we'll have a market of 250 million. Everything was going to be lovely in the garden. I opposed them. I said,

'You'll find things get worse. You'll lose your independence, be sub-ordinated to decrees made by a Commission, which is undemocratic, self-appointing . . . ' We had a great deal of trouble in the Labour Party because of my attitude. I was not only in opposition, but aggressively in opposition. I was convinced I was right.

Can you get out? How are we to escape from it all? I put it this way: it's as difficult to escape from the Common Market as to escape from the House of Lords. [*By this, Manny surely meant escape from the problem of what to do about the Upper House.*]

It is possible to escape — [with] a great many complications. Should we come out, or should we reform it along the lines some of us have suggested? I would abolish the Common Agricultural Policy. I would make it clear we're going to have no interference with our fishing rights. I would make it clear that, although we're associated on economic sub-jects they [the EEC] would not be able to decide matters which are essentially British.

J.D. "There is the question of how far we could withdraw without unilaterally abrogating our treaty obligations. Is there an element of national morality involved?"
Well, that would seem to be the case. But we have in the past abrogated treaties. We reneged on them when we found them not working to our satisfaction. I don't believe it's physically possible to withdraw, although we'll become more independent, we'd have to face problems just as severe as those that now exist . . .

J.D. "In the long run, do you think it would be in our national interest to withdraw?"
The general answer is the one I gave to the Labour Conference: inter-national co-operation as represented by the shambles of the United Nations is of little value. The kind of international co-operation I want is a body not so much concerned with the political aspects as the industrial and commercial ones. Commodities, prices, deliveries, quality of goods — all these are very important aspects of trade. For that purpose, we need a body of expert industrialists and financiers — with as few politicians as possible. Not allowing politics to intrude at all if they can be excluded. Essentially, a body that looks at the world as it IS. [Desirable results] will not be achieved by the present international organizations. They're obsessed by politics.

J.D. "But any such organizations can only be set up by politicians."
Politicians will always want to intervene. I don't want any of that . . . We CAN keep them out.

49

George V

I was Secretary for Mines in the first Labour Government [1923–4]. George V was the Sailor King. One day MacDonald, the Prime Minister, said, 'There's been a very unusual request. The King wants to see you.' I said, 'Why?' He said, 'I don't know. Very unusual: the King only sees Cabinet Ministers. But if the King wants to see you, you'll have to go.'

I go back to my department and I ask to see my Permanent Secretary, and say 'The King wants to see me.' 'Oh,' he said, 'I'd better consult the Lord Chamberlain.' He comes back later on and says, 'That's all right, but the Minister must wear [formal] black clothes.' I said, 'I haven't got any black clothes.' 'You can hire them,' he says. I said, 'You mean, me hire clothes! I've had some trouble in my time — but I haven't needed to hire clothes!' So they take it back, and the Lord Chamberlain decides I can go in a lounge suit.

Then the question arose about going there. Nowadays, a junior Minister gets a car; no such thing then. Our salary was £1500 a year. I'd no car, so I said, 'What am I to do?' My Private Secretary said, 'You just walk across.'

I walked to the gate of Buckingham Palace. When I got there, the policeman said 'Where are you going?' I said, 'I've come to see the King.' He said, 'Cross the quadrangle and ask the official.' So I did. An equerry came down — an officer, an airman — and then I go up and shake hands — and the King started on me.

What he wanted to see me about was — he was concerned about shipping, and he knew I was connected with the Seamen's Union. So he wanted to get my views — what conditions were like and so on — was there going to be any trouble. Matters of that sort. That's all. He never offered me a drink, never offered me a cigarette. He just yelled his head off. I managed to get a few words in before I left.

One of the sequels was years later when I got the Companionship of Honour. When you get the CH you go to see the Queen. It's not done in public. I see the Queen, in her private rooms, and she asks me about her grandfather: 'How did you find him?' So I told her exactly what I've told you — but I said he was very pleasant about it. She laughed her head off.

* * *

It was remarkable that King George V — it's not well known — how often he interfered in political matters. The monarchy, after Queen Victoria, seldom bothered. King Edward VII didn't bother: he was enjoying himself. Still more remarkable was his [George V's] interest in the Irish problems. In fact, on one occasion he made a statement on Ireland . . . and when he went in his carriage through London, people were applauding him for what he said. He wanted a united Ireland. He was always getting on at Lloyd George to do something. He dabbled in politics more than any other [modern] monarch. When he heard about someone being appointed a Minister, he would sometimes object.

J.D. "He was constitutionally entitled to object . . .'
It was not what was expected.

Personal History

Discovery Of Books

I found a better source of education; Glasgow Public Library. I would remain there until turned out at ten. The daring theories of evolution by Darwin I found absorbing. I read works on zoology, geology and palaeontology, and was encouraged to study specimens of stuffed animals, rocks and fossils in museums.

In 1902 my father was offered management of a clothing factory in South Shields and returned to the town. I remained in Glasgow. Most of my spare money had for some years been spent on books. By searching in second-hand bookshops and junk barrows, I accumulated about 250 volumes. I had broadened my taste. I collected works by Dickens and Trollope, Meredith and Hardy. Keats and Burns were my favourite poets. There were scores of scientific and philosophical works . . .

My father said he needed my help in South Shields, and I took my precious library with me. The old disputes began again and after a year I decided I would return to Glasgow. I had been much attracted by a boxing booth, and would have joined it except for knowing Glasgow was a home I liked. I had no money for the fare, and food and lodging until I found work. As a result, I was compelled to sell my library. South Shields had few lovers of literature. After pushing my library around on a barrow without getting an offer, a bookseller grumpily agreed to buy them at twopence per volume.

Government

Devolution

On the administrative side, I'm in favour of regional organization. I wasn't too happy about the Scottish devolution business: in my opinion it was based on emotion. It wasn't a practical or logical approach — as I'd always understood the movement's attitude to be when I was younger. I supported Home Rule in my first election address in 1918 [in Scotland]. Scottish Home Rule wasn't then a matter of emotion, but caused by the attitude of the government which disregarded or ignored the Scots.

By regional organization, I mean the sort they have in Australia — federation. What I would do is this. You start off with a government which is elected, and the government's got the supreme authority in certain directions — foreign affairs and defence. Why? Because those are the primary elements in maintaining security . . . Apart from that, there's the question of taxation: should be a matter for the State. But when it comes to how you deal with housing, roads, land and its development — local matters — those are matters for the regions. I don't mean parish councils: I mean much as we have in Scotland with Strathclyde, which is a vast area — though whether it's properly managed is another matter. And they [regional governments] would be endowed with certain powers.

J.D. "Would Scotland have its own Parliament?"
Scotland would be divided into regions.

J.D. "Those would be responsible to Edinburgh or Westminster?"
Everyone would be responsible to Westminster, all the regional governments of the UK. I wouldn't have a government in Edinburgh, but occasionally have the regional authorities meeting together in Edinburgh to discuss some problem common to all the regions.

If there are to be regional governments in Scotland, the same must apply to England — Northumberland–Durham–Yorkshire, and on the other side Lancashire–Cheshire — and so on. Same with Wales: there's a vast difference between North and South Wales. These regions should have a degree of autonomy. One thing is certain: the people of North-east [England] will object if Scotland gets devolution — 'What about our problems?' [they'll say].

An 'Imperial' Parliament

I'm not sure we couldn't associate the idea of autonomous regional organizations with the creation of an 'imperial' parliament. From the particular regions, twenty to forty members could be elected by proportional representation. This parliament could deal with 'imperial' matters; wouldn't interfere with local affairs. I wouldn't have too much of that.

Proportional Representation
I have supported proportional representation. I don't become enthusiastic about it because I've got reservations, and I've annoyed the Liberals by saying so. They thought they'd dragged me into it, would have liked me on their side. I want PR because I think it's more democratic than the present system. But I don't want it for the purpose of creating a situation where one small party holds the balance of power; that's got to be avoided.

I've previously suggested that no decision to remove a government on a vote of censure should be operated unless with seventy-five per cent of MPs voting one way or the other. But PR, provided you get the right type — there are various forms — even the transferable vote would be all right, although it's not completely democratic — I'd accept that.

* * *

I'm not against coalitions. I didn't like them at first. But if we decided to adopt the autonomous regions notion, then I don't object to coalitions.

Local Government
There are many councillors who don't do any work at all — just collect expenses. I don't like the notion of a councillor attending so many meetings simply as a way of getting a living.

J.D. "There's so much corruption in present local politics."
There's far too much — and I know it exists.

* * *

When it comes down to brass tacks, do you think ANY of the governments we've had in the last fifty, sixty, one hundred years have contributed much to the well-being of the people of this country?

The Grayson Mystery

A leading member of the early Labour Party was Victor Grayson, a fine orator, for whom many forecast an important political future. He completely vanished in 1920 — creating a sensation. What is generally accepted as happening is that Grayson was drinking in a London hotel bar when he was called away because of an alleged mix-up over his luggage. He was never seen again by any living witness. In recent years, Manny was approached over a play and a TV programme about Grayson: nothing came of these projects so far as he was concerned. However, a new slant on this peculiar event was given to him by an apparently impeccable source.

A Mystery Deepens

In 1979, when I was at the Brighton Labour Conference, I was approached by a lady who gave her name as Mrs Watkins — she was Grayson's daughter — an elderly lady, with her husband, who was a retired bank manager. She told me what she knew . . . but I probably knew as much as she did. She wanted to write a book about him [her father], but she'd approached publishers who said there's nothing conclusive about it and only if there was would it be worthwhile. But some people now involved in the arrangements [for a book] consider that the mystery — the fact that there is a mystery — can be used.

J.D. "I can see that. Was she the only child?"
I don't know. That's all.

J.D. "They write here [a feature in The Observer*] that he may have been murdered on the orders of Maundy Gregory, the famous charlatan."*
That's pure guesswork. [According to his daughter] what happened to him in the end — apparently, when he came back from Australia or New Zealand after the war, he then lived with a lady described by Mrs Watkins as 'a benevolent person' — whatever that may mean. One night, a car came to the place where he lived and took him away. That was the end of him. I asked Mrs Watkins what she thought had happened. She said one idea was that he worked for the British Secret Service for some reason.

J.D. "Is that likely, from what you knew of him?"
Under pressure. Or he defected to the Russians, which is much more likely. That was the end: she knew no more. No one else knows anything more. All sorts of people have been working on it. I have all sorts of requests made for what I know about Victor Grayson. I'm sick and tired of it.

Health

Will you fill your pipe, and I'll get a drink.

Manny said he had just experienced a twinge of gout, a subject of personal interest to me. I said I had suffered for years, but seemed to have bested it.

I'll tell you my experience. I was living in Hampstead Garden Suburb at the time. One morning I got out of bed and thought I'd sprained my ankle. I arranged a car to take me to the House of Commons. When I got there, Colonel [later Lord] Wigg — he was my unpaid Parliamentary Secretary — suggested I go to Westminster Hospital. They diagnosed gout. At the time I was just about fifty. They decided I must rest, take pills. I had a lot of gout trouble . . . then it disappeared. Now, every six months or so, it'll come back. It's possible to deal with it.

Why did I get gout? I was then at the War Office. While I was there, I had lunches every day, dinner every day, cocktail parties — and I drank wine. That was just the cause of it. For thirty-five — forty — years I've never touched wine. Even when invited to the Vintage Dinner. The waiter knows me. He comes over and says, 'Lord Shinwell, shall I get you some whisky?' I say, 'Yes, please.'

* * *

The only complaint Manny admitted to was occasional bouts of exhaustion.

I sleep so badly. I've been advised to take sleeping pills: very rarely do I take one. The next day, I feel so drowsy, so I don't take them. The result is, I do most of my reading at night. Last night I was reading from about two until seven in the morning. I was reading Samuel Butler's *The Way of All Flesh*, which is a terrible book to read if you want to go to sleep.

J.D. 'Do you have a nap in the afternoon?'

No. I take very little breakfast. Sometimes I have a bit of lunch here [at home], hardly worth talking about. Then, when I go down to the Chamber and listen to a debate for a little while or ask a question, they mumble so much I decide I'm not going to sleep in the Chamber, so I go to the library — but I can't sleep there at all. I'll tell you when I can sleep. When I get back here at night and have some dinner — never a very heavy dinner — I don't eat much — I go off to sleep until nine or ten o'clock. I go to bed about ten and I can continue to sleep for one or two hours — three o'clock's the latest. I don't sleep a wink after then.

. . . Occasionally, I'm on the phone to my consultant. I say, 'I don't like this way I'm feeling.' He says, 'Take a drop of whisky.' I say, 'I've taken some.' He says, 'Take more!'

Smoking

I'm not smoking as much as I used to. I used to smoke five ounces a week. I doubt if I now smoke two. I smoke a cigar occasionally, at night: I only smoke half of it. I've never smoked cigarettes. I started to smoke a pipe when I was thirteen, a clay pipe. I remember it made me sick. I became a pipe-smoker because my father was a pipe-smoker.

In January, 1984, Manny, intervening in exchanges in the Lords on statistics on deaths from smoking, elicited from Lord Glenarthur, Under Secretary for Health, an admission that it was cigarettes which were the prime culprits. Two months later, when a peer suggested smoking should be totally banned on buses, Manny said he was becoming "a bit aggravated" at efforts to interfere with "civilized existence."

* * *

I've lost my taste for luncheon and that sort of thing. If I'm sitting at a luncheon and talking to people, I don't consume my food and sometimes I feel more anxious to have a drop of whisky than anything else.

J.D. "You can have what you want."
I DO!

House of Lords

I have to confess something. There are some people on our front bench I can't stand. The palaver, the pomposity, the pretence at being clever — I see through it so easily.

J.D. "What's your idea of a second chamber? Some Labour MPs want a unicameral government."
If they decide to abolish the House of Lords, they must have an alternative. Why do I say that? When some members of the Labour Party talk about leaving discretion entirely in the hands of the House of Commons, I point this out: time and again the Commons deal with legislation

which calls for amendment. You must have a second opinion on any [important] topic. Where would you get that second opinion? If you can't get it from the House of Lords, who have no authority, but recommend, if you can't have that, you must have something in its place. You could, of course, create a commission of some kind, some members of the Commons and others, and say, 'We'll leave it to a Select Committee.' A Select Committee could come to a decision by a majority — eventually.

What I would do with the House of Lords is very simple. I would reduce the numbers on the Conservative benches, and that is acceptable even to many members on the Tory side. We agree about that. Heredity is not the issue. Many should not be there at all. Many of the life peers on the other [Labour] side need not be there. They ought to correct the imbalance, because otherwise we know that on [nearly] every division, the Conservatives are going to win. In fact, I sometimes find myself going to the Division lobby and saying to a colleague, 'I feel like being on the winning side tonight, so I think I'll go in with the Tories!' I'd like to put that right.

I would do something about the speeches. Some are very good, but they're all read, prepared speeches. Mine, of course, are NEVER read. What I would do is this: I would not hold a debate without a conclusion. Now, there are any number of debates in the Lords, where you get some wonderful speeches, but, as I've said more than once, 'What do we DO?' We've got all the famous economists there, many scientists, educationalists, and at the end, when we finish the debate — no motion. Nothing. I say, you've got to come to a decision. Then you'd count for something. It doesn't follow that the House of Commons should accept your decision, but at least you've expressed an opinion. Otherwise, it's just a talking-shop. I don't want that.

Those are the reforms I would make. When we talk about reform, I say you only need reform in procedure. Another thing: they [the Tories] appoint people on committees — and so on. A bit of a scandal. I'd put a stop to all that. No one should be appointed to a committee without consultation with the Opposition. Otherwise, it's a matter of the government doing exactly as they like.

These are simple things that could be done. I'd like to see the House of Lords as it is, reduced in number of members, with no more authority than it now possesses, but with its speeches AND conclusions.

J.D. "Who would decide who'd constitute this reduced House of Lords?"
It could be done in a simple way. All it requires is introduction of legislation calling for a reduction in members. There are over a thousand at the

moment. I would reduce that to three hundred, perhaps three-fifty. Those selected should be appointed, not elected.

J.D. "So you don't believe in an elected upper chamber, a Senate."
I don't believe in a House of Lords that has authority. It's an advisory body. It's sometimes described as a revising body: I'm against that.

J.D. "Should the peers have any delaying powers at all?"
I don't think they should, except on some fundamental issue . . . if there's a constitutional issue, one that involves the transfer of an industry to the State or vice versa — or some piece of legislation that is of a fundamental character affecting the country as a whole — or on a matter of defence . . . There ought to be more consultation between the two Houses of Parliament.

My suggestion is that the Commons and Lords, reduced in numbers, should meet together occasionally to discuss some topic. That's a feasible proposition . . . have fifty or so from each, having a discussion.

J.D. "Are you suggesting there are too many MPs, that the Commons should be reduced as well?"
Yes, you could increase the size of constituencies and have fewer members of Parliament. They say they are overworked. I don't believe it.

J.D. "I don't think anyone else does!"
They're overworked in functions, of sorts. And some don't do anything at all. The same applies to the Lords. Some only turn up every six months — make a speech, and off they go.

J.D. "Would you retain some hereditary peers?"
So long as they have ability.

J.D. "Who decides?"
If you get someone who's a prominent industrialist, with scientific knowledge, a reputation — by all means don't lose him. Even if it's someone who's a great orator — for a change — have someone like that. I wouldn't like to lose Lord Soper. I don't agree with him a bit — he always brings in the Christian religion — but I like to listen to him.

J.D. 'To repeat: who would actually sit in the Lords?"
That's decided by the Prime Minister and a committee.

J.D. "That's what happens at the moment. Looking ahead, are you

saying there'd be life peerages to give someone an honour, but not necessarily with a seat in the House of Lords?"
I'm not saying that. I wouldn't worry much about such things. A prominent industrialist, a trade union leader — we need those sorts of people. It must be flexible. [*Manny then seemed to go back on his rejection of non-voting peers, adding*]: You could have a large number of the peerage who were not members of the House of Lords.

J.D. "As you have hereditary Scottish and Irish peers who are non-representative?"
These are very easy problems to solve. They are not really problems at all. The point is: do you need a second Chamber at all? For what purpose? I want a second Chamber. I want it for considering the legislation that comes before the Commons and is sent to us, in order to ensure it represents public opinion. Then it goes back to the Commons, and they really decide. They're the elected democratic body.

J.D. "Unless I read it wrong, Benn and his kind. . ."
. . . want to abolish the whole thing. Actually he doesn't go as far as that. Heffer — he's against any second Chamber. He's not saying much at the moment — and that's no loss to the country! [*Mr Heffer has since made up for any temporary loss of voice.*]

The general opinion in the country is that the House of Lords must be retained, but in the way I've indicated. That would have widespread approval.

When I've talked about it, I've sometimes made fun of it. They ask, 'Why then did you go to the Lords?' I answer, 'Where else is there to go?'

* * *

Manny complained that the popular press gave scant attention to sensible debates in the Lords.
If it's pornography, they do. But normal political subjects are hardly ever mentioned.

J.D. "A number of bishops sit in the Lords: good idea?"
I wonder myself whether that's necessary. Sometimes their speeches are valuable. But there's always a certain direction in them which, of course, makes the speeches seem concerned with a fixed idea, a dramatic expression, which is incapable of argument. For example [some bishop] speaks in the Lords and expresses an opinion which is of a theological character. It's very rarely any member gets up and refutes what he's

said. It would seem to be improper. Therefore, I would prevent the bishops from being there at all. But if someone suggested that, there'd be a terrible row. They'd say, 'That's revolution!'

But solving one problem creates another. If we decided to reform the House of Lords and have no bishops, the poor bishops wouldn't know what to do — less opportunity to come to London!

* * *

Every now and then you look around the House of Lords and wonder, 'Where's so-and-so?' And you're told he's dead. They don't announce it. In the House of Commons, they do. If a Member dies, the Speaker will always refer to the honourable Member who has just passed away. If he's a very prominent Member, they'll have tributes.

In the House of Lords you can just die and no one pays attention. I sit often in the library if I'm not interested in a debate, and I look around and wonder where old so-and-so is. Sometimes I make inquiries — one has to be careful about that — I make inquiries from an attendant: 'Have you seen Lord so-and-so?' 'No, sir, he's passed away.'

I wonder, if anything happens to me . . . twenty-four hours after you've gone — no one has heard of you. There never was such a person! [Hearty chuckles.] It's a terrible thought!

Personal History

Small Triumph: Big Disaster

The two guineas (210p) I received [from the sale of books in South Shields] were my sole capital as I made what I thought would be my final departure from home. The reason why Glasgow was such a magnet was that I had a sweetheart there. At the time of returning to Scotland, we had no idea of marrying for some time. A year later, with my nineteenth birthday at hand and having a good job, we decided to marry, against the wishes of both families.

By this time, I had acquired an interest in Socialism. Although I found the idea attractive, I had little time for those who expected to put the world right by political action. Pursuit of science, as outlined by H. G. Wells, was to my mind the key to a better civilization. [Neil McLean, later a long-serving MP] told me [after a meeting] I had an abysmal ignorance of economics. As a result I got hold of a pamphlet by Karl Marx. I was not the first young man to discover Marx is hard going. I read and re-read that pamphlet and eventually extracted worth-while material for a discussion. In due course I got a chance to see if I could expound Marxist views, my adversary a theological speaker. At the end of the debate a collection was taken. To my amazement my opponent handed over ten shillings (50p) as my share. It seemed I was 'in politics'.

I ventured to think my wife had good reason to be proud of a husband not unknown to the working class of Glasgow as a political speaker, had a good job, and had been able to furnish a single room as the bridal home. The proverbial fall soon came.

Within a month of my marriage the usual slump arrived in the clothing trade. I was a new employee and agitator for workers' rights. I was dismissed. There was no unemployment relief. Our savings were nil. For three terrible months I could find no work. On our first New Year's Eve together we were literally penniless. We sold almost everything we possessed except the clothes we stood in. Eventually I had to admit defeat and return to South Shields. My wife remained in Glasgow, a spur to me to return as soon as I could. I achieved this after a few months.

Israel

[*Manny mentioned the internal situation*]. The religious element can be very troublesome, as fanatical as [the Palestinians]. What Israel has got is first-class fighters. Indeed if one reads history, not only biblical but associated with the Old Testament, one discovers that their [the Jews'] capacity for fighting was amazing for thousands and thousands of years. They were always fighting somebody. And when they were defeated, they always recovered; even when they were refugees in Babylon for hundreds of years, they recovered.

In addition to that — although I don't pretend I'm wholly aware of the details — I am certain — and I was certain almost twenty years ago — that the Israelis have the Bomb. I remember going to the Weizmann Institute [of Science] when I was visiting Israel as Secretary of State for War and I was convinced in my discussions with some of the scientists, that they had got it.

J.D. "They couldn't have tested it."

There's a great deal of mystery there. It's assumed you can't test the efficiency — if one can use that term — of an atom bomb except in a desert or in the ocean . . . I don't agree with that. It depends on what you're trying to test. If you want to test its power, its capacity for devastation, there are ways and means scientists can devise.

But I don't think the Israelis are afraid of their capacity to deal with the situation, with Syria or Iraq or any of the countries round about. They're very doubtful about Egypt, though . . . Trouble with Egypt could cause Egypt to become a satellite of the Soviet Union.

J.D. "And Gaddafi?"

I think he's on the way out. That's my impression. It's not him — it's the Russians operating all the time. They'll get their own back on the Egyptians for the expulsion of their advisers. In addition to which, there's an economic situation in Egypt which could easily cause a revolution.

Manny made a very accurate prediction of what occurred in Lebanon in 1983–4.

It's a paradox. The Saudis are afraid of communism, yet encourage Russia to support countries like Syria, Iraq, and the Palestinians. Russia has built up such an arsenal of munitions that she can afford to give some away.

* * *

I've done a lot for Israel privately. I was very friendly with Golda Meir. I knew Ben Gurion [Israel's first premier]. I helped them, but I've never been one of them.

Labour Party

The Labour Party, if it abandons any of the principles on which it was founded, will not win, and will not deserve to win, because we would be winning under false pretences. That's no good. Far better to be defeated than to adopt a middle of the road policy which can be left either to the Tory party or to some other organisation. It's not for the Labour Party. I recognize that if you are producing a policy about which there has

been a great deal of discussion in the party — never mind people outside the party, I don't bother about them — we [must] always get back to the principles on which it was founded.
(*See also* SOCIALISM)

Danger From the Unions
I warned them [the Labour Party] the greatest danger is not the SDP [Alliance] or the Tory party — the greatest danger would be that the trade union movement, upon which the Labour Party depends for its finance, might decide to hive off from the political section of the Labour movement and produce an organization of its own, based not on parliamentary democracy, but concerned with unconstitutional, direct action — which would be dangerous for the Labour movement and disastrous for the country.

It nearly happened many years ago when a number of trade union leaders, dissatisfied with the activities of Labour MPs, decided to create a trade union organization. But it was prevented by Arthur Henderson. The same thing could happen again. Then the Labour Party would be faced by an organization much more powerful than the party itself. We can't afford that.

J.D. "It would often appear to an outsider that the Parliamentary Labour Party is split between what you might call social-democrats — not SDP *— and a section which is almost marxist — almost irreconcilable although nominally members of the same party."*

Recurrence of Party Splits
Here I must return to what I've frequently said: this sort of thing has happened before. I'll give you perhaps the classic example. When Hugh Gaitskell became leader, he wished to expunge Clause 4 from the party's constitution — the nationalization of means of production, distribution and exchange — which had been introduced by Sidney Webb [Lord Passfield] and a few others in 1918 and accepted by the party. But that didn't suit Gaitskell: he wanted something more modern, a middle of the road party. We were back to square one, back to where we started, back to whether we should proceed along Socialist lines or adopt a middle-road policy.

[I said] that to proceed with a middle of the road policy would be pointless. It could never enable us to achieve our objectives . . . What are we seeking to achieve . . .? A bit of Left, a bit of Right — bits of this and that?

J.D. "If in any party you get an obvious split, it's got to be resolved by one side winning the battle, hasn't it?"

For me — it may be different for the ambitious — I'm not concerned with |simply| winning an election. What I am concerned about is to gain power to enable us to create a system of society in accord with Socialist principles . . . Otherwise, what do we gain?

Leadership

When I'm asked about leaders of the Labour Party, I say we've never had a leader I would regard as satisfactory. We've never had a leader with the right sense of direction. He was always influenced by his own personal desires or by what HE thought was best for the nation.

This from Manny's resumé of a speech he made at a Labour conference:

Leaders are of no consequence, and therefore the lust for leadership is of no consequence. And whoever becomes leader is in a very embarrassing position. Don't get the idea that generals win battles, or even field marshals . . . it's soldiers, the rank and file — YOU — who win battles. So you shouldn't worry about leaders.

I exceeded my time. I paid no attention to the |warning| lights: I never do!

* * *

I've never had the slightest desire for leadership, never felt I wished to be leader of the party, though it was suggested more than once. I am concerned, still concerned, with objectives.

J.D. "Don't you think many of these people [politicians] pay lip service to objectives, while power is their main objective?"

They're ambitious, of course. I've said nearly all MPs want to be leaders, consider themselves potential leaders. Let them enjoy themselves! If they think so highly of themselves, I'm not protesting!

Humiliating Squabbles

Though the following referred to the squabbles over the deputy leadership conflict in the Labour party in the autumn of 1981, Manny's comments retain a certain topicality.

I listened to three prominent members of the party addressing an audience who had gathered to hear their respective opinions. As a member of the Labour Party — the oldest surviving member of the party — I felt humiliated that prominent people in the party to which I belong should have presented themselves at a meeting pleading to be elected to the deputy leadership. This was canvassing of the worst possible kind. To have sought the aid of friends, or even of enemies, to enable them to achieve their ambition: that one can understand. But to expose themselves in public in the way they did — I found it a humiliation I had never experienced before. There was a comment by someone at that gathering which expressed my view; 'Why should we worry about a deputy leader anyway?' I repeat the question: why? what for? To provide a post for some member, to enable him to get on the first rung of the ladder to becoming leader? What contribution is that man going to make to solving any of our [party] problems? All it was doing was to create fresh problems.

I felt disgusted, almost disgraced, that it should happen. Many things have happened to me in the political arena, much of which I disliked; even things have happened for which I was responsible which perhaps should have not occured — we're not all angels — but that [meeting] was the worst ever. It was unspeakable. It did not matter in the least which of those three was elected deputy leader . . . [*Manny's indignation made him query whether he should remain a party member — seventy-seven years after he joined the old Independent Labour Party.*] . . . I propose not to trust any of those who exposed themselves, but to trust the good sense of the British public and pay no attention to all the policies that have been adumbrated recently, but not yet realized. As I've said and written, 'Changes are inevitable.' The changes that will occur will be probably quite different from the changes that have been suggested by any of those three exponents.

True Socialist Policies

We are now faced in this country with three main parties: the Conservatives, Labour, and the SDP [Liberal Alliance]. The Conservatives wish to maintain the present situation, and improve upon it, to satisfy their ambitions to make more profits for industry by cutting back on nationalization . . . That we understand. The policy of the SDP [Liberals] is a middle of the road policy which is bound in the end to be fruitless because it can't achieve what is necessary to deal with existing problems.

J.D. "Attractive to the voters, though."

But not a remedy. And on the Labour side you've got the Socialist policy. What I have said [in an article for *Labour Weekly*] is this: the Labour Party can't win the next election [*they did not*] if they abandon their Socialist principles, upon which the party was founded. They must go forward with a definite Socialist policy.

Now, as regards the internal state of the party — re-selection of members . . . whether we should remain in the Common Market . . . even the question of unilateralism or multilateralism — these are all subjects on which we should not be too dogmatic. There should be working parties on such topics to produce blue-prints to satisfy electors before we introduce legislation.

Rhetoric v. Reality

Benn — no one's more critical of him than I am, for personal, for all sorts of reasons. [But] you can trust him. He's honest, not working for himself — working for the party. I wouldn't mind Benn being leader of the Labour Party, not in the least — I know them.

J.D. "Just to put a point as a member of the public — apolitical myself, not belonging to any party — I see Benn as a frightener. Isn't he too much of a bogeyman to get power?"
My dear sir, let me give you an illustration. Stafford Cripps — an intellectual, university man, great barrister, rich — he cried, 'Put the red flag on Buckingham Palace!' Then in 1949 — devaluation twice, austerity and all the rest of it — that's what Stafford DID.

J.D. "But he wasn't leader."
He was worse than that — he was behind the party leader, who was ill. Attlee was ill, and Bevin — Ernie Bevin — wasn't too well himself. Stafford was worse than Crossman — his interventions were notorious — on almost anything.

This party of ours, the party to which I belong — time and again it's devoted itself to men who would come out and pretend to be revolutionaries, who would fight to the death on behalf of their principles — only for it to be discovered that they had no principles, merely self-interest.

* * *

It's when they'll be facing hard facts that they [Labour MPs] will realize what a mistake they've made [by passing numerous fancy resolutions in conference]. But what will happen? Do you think they'll resign? Not at all. Do you think they'll say . . . 'We find we can't carry out the policy the National Executive Council decided upon.'? Are they going to resign — give up their jobs? What — at X thousands a year and secretaries and perks and all the rest of it? They're going to hang on as long as they can.

With a majority of three, we were able to carry on when I was chairman of the Parliamentary Labour Party — because of me. Because I would have people brought before me — Mikardo, Jenkins, who's now in the Lords, Atkinson, treasurer of the party — because of speeches they made outside. The Chief Whip would inform me of what they'd said, and I would say, 'Well, deal with them.' And he'd say, 'No, you deal with them.' I can see them now. I'd say to Mikardo, 'You can't go and make a speech like that. Better make up your mind — get out, or else . . .' that sort of thing. Discipline, authority — I've said it over and over again — you can't run a party except on those lines.

Personal History

A Stockbroker Manqué

If, instead of going to South Shields to meet my father who had started a business there, I had remained in London and gone to school, had more education — I should probably have gone into business, and ended up on the Stock Exchange, and made half a million — at least! But making money never occurred to me.

Either that, or I might have done very well in sport. One of the two. I can't imagine living a quiet life. It might be I entered the political arena because I wanted excitement, needed excitement.

* * *

It's a curious thing — it's always difficult to get across to people — they always think you're out for money. And if you do make a bit, by writing, say, or investment . . . I'm not bad at that, by the way, although I've no knowledge of finance. That's part of the racial characteristic, maybe. I never was bothered about money, though I often found myself in difficulties.

Lloyd George

I had some association with Lloyd George during the First World War. It arose because of my connection with the Scottish Trade Union movement, when Lloyd George was Minister for Munitions, before he became Prime Minister, when Asquith was still PM. Lloyd George at that time was exceedingly active, industrious to a degree. Now, in the west of Scotland, during World War One, practically the whole working population was engaged in making munitions. We hadn't got to the tank period. We were only on the fringe of aircraft production, but we were certainly producing vessels of war — not as many as we would have liked. The government was in trouble during the whole of the war through scarcity of vessels.

Now LG had gone to the Tyne to talk to the munition workers, shipyard workers, because the Tyne and the Clyde were the two most important shipbuilding areas. When we heard he'd gone to Tyne, a demand came from an organization known as the Clyde Workers' Committee, which was militant, revolutionary, for Lloyd George to visit the Clyde. He was asked to come up, and refused. The government had introduced dilution into munition establishments; that means people were introduced who were unskilled. This was regarded as likely to erode the strength and influence of skilled engineers and shipwrights. It was threatened that if Lloyd George did not come up to discuss dilution [there would be trouble] — the workers were anxious to increase production, no doubt about that. Eventually he decided to come, under pressure. Instead of talking to the munition workers in a businesslike fashion, consulting with them, listening to their suggestions, which were designed towards greater efficiency and production, he talked about 'a land fit for heroes to live in'. That was the theme of every one of his speeches.

Well, it was decided he should come up again [now as Prime Minister], since the first meeting had proved abortive. He would address a demonstration and meeting in Glasgow in the largest of our halls. I sat on the platform. He did precisely what he'd done on the previous occasion. He made one of his elegant speeches. He was a scintillating orator — humorous, witty, capable of repartee . . . So that meeting was abortive, too.

A Visit To Churt

Clem Davies was parliamentary leader of the Liberal Party [during World War II] — kind of 'king-maker', great behind-the-scenes man — he was a great commercial lawyer — never himself got into a government position . . . He came to me one day. I was prominent at the time, having refused a job under Churchill, and [he] said, 'I want you to go down to meet Lloyd George.' I said, 'What about?' He said, 'I think it would be very useful if he came up and fortified the Opposition.' I said, 'We haven't got an Opposition.' He said, 'You know — the awkward squad — Nye Bevan, Silverman and a few like that. Try to get him to come up and take charge.' I said, 'You're asking me: you know I've always had trouble with him — the Glasgow trouble, the Clyde trouble.' But he didn't know much about it. He said, 'You're just the man to do it. Far better you should do it than someone who's friendly with him.' I couldn't understand that myself, but I said, 'Oh, well, I'll go by train.'

I go to Chertsey, and at the exit a lady came up, Miss Stevenson, and she said Lloyd George was going round the estate. I was ushered into a room — large room with huge plate-glass windows . . . I could see him coming, dressed in a cloak — a sort of rainproof thing — with one of his managers. He came into the room and shook hands and welcomed me. After a minute or two he asked me if I would like a drink. I said, 'Yes, that's a good idea.' 'What d'you want?' he said. I said, 'A drop of Scotch.' He said, 'If you take Scotch, you have soda with it, but if you have Irish whiskey you take water.' I never knew that before! I said, 'We don't want to embarrass the government. We want to win this war if we can. But we know there are difficulties, and it's suggested you come up and fortify the Opposition by suggesting things out of your own experience. We don't mind at all if you take charge of the Opposition bench.' He said right away, 'I've had my war. This is Winnie's war.' He wouldn't have it.

Time came for lunch. There were only the three of us. Apparently he had thought of a new kind of economy soup in order to save money. It was an ordinary kind of soup.* I don't think I had anything else.

* * *

J.D. 'At one time during the war, Lloyd George had the reputation of being rather defeatist."
He was. He didn't think we would win.

Lloyd George and Hitler
I have been re-reading the biography of Lloyd George — and particularly that part of it where Lloyd George went to Germany on the suggestion of Ribbentrop [when he was ambassador to Britain], and met Hitler at Berchtesgaden. He was full of praise for Hitler.

---

* *Two recipes for 'Churt Soups' (named for Lloyd George's estate) were given in* Conflict Without Malice. *They are indeed 'ordinary'.*

J.D. "At that time, most people who actually met Hitler, liked him."
The same applied to Lansbury [veteran Socialist] and several others . . .
But why did Lloyd George, a man of high intelligence and experience,
allow himself to succumb to Hitler's blandishments? It is a very interesting study — because when I think of LG and how harsh he could be, for
example to the munition workers on the Clydeside during the First
World War, and how harsh he could be to those who didn't agree with
him politically and in his relations with some of his colleagues, one
wonders how he could be so emotional in his association with Hitler.

J.D. "The Welsh are rather emotional."
You're saying something now that leads me to be a little suspicious of
the Welsh. Do you mean they exude charm to such an extent that one
has to be very cautious about them?

J.D. "I'd be extremely cautious."
I've known so many Welshmen and Welshwomen I'd hestitate to agree
with that. If you take the example of Lloyd George: he was a man who
could be so austere and harsh and firm in his views, in his assessments of
other people — yet he fell for him [Hitler].

Ramsay MacDonald

I first met MacDonald when, as a member of the Glasgow Trades
Council, I'd go to the House of Commons. During the First World War,
MacDonald [who favoured peace by negotiation] came up several times
to Glasgow. One time he was coming up and a meeting was arranged at
the Charing Cross Hall in Sauchiehall Street, and in the preceding week
in the newspapers there was a great deal of talk about an organization
called the Scottish Patriotic Federation who threatened to break up the
MacDonald meeting.

I read this before the meeting on a Friday night. I didn't pay any
attention. So I go up to the meeting and when I crossed the street I saw a
big crowd outside the hall. So I went over and pushed my way through.
A couple of stewards were holding the glass doors against the crowd . . .
I was talking to MacDonald for a minute or two and then there was a

noise outside. I went to the head of the stairs and saw where the stewards were holding the doors there was someone with his head between the doors. He was the chairman of this organization [the Scottish Patriotic Federation]. I only saw his face. What was I to do? I didn't want them to break up my meeting. So on impulse I ran down the steps and hit the man and got the doors closed. I went up, and no one said anything, and I opened the meeting. I didn't agree with MacDonald. I never did agree with him about this. I was in favour of prosecuting the war in the most vigorous forms possible. I was doing some work for the government at the time.

Anyway, we got through the meeting and we went down. The crowd had started to disperse. There was a large number of policemen outside. One of the detectives whom I knew from my work in the docks said, 'You're in trouble.' 'Why, what's up?' I asked. I was a Town Councillor and president of the Trades Council at that time. He said, 'It's alleged you hit a man with a lead pipe. I have to report it.'

I went off. I didn't bother about it. On the Monday I got a summons to appear before the stipendiary magistrate for hitting this man. Amongst the witnesses was this man with a bandage. He was asked if he was responsible for what appeared in the *Evening News* on Friday night [about the intention to disrupt the meeting]. He didn't deny it. He'd come along to break up the meeting because they were patriots and against that sort of thing. The magistrate summed up on the basis of the evidence. I remember the language quite well: 'Here's a case where a man threatens to break up a meeting and then accuses the chairman of the meeting of having assaulted him. This is grotesque, fantastic. I dismiss it.' No one tried to break up any more of my meetings.

MacDonald wasn't happy about it. He disliked any kind of violence.

A Caution from Mac

There was another occasion — some meeting of the seamen — I was addressing, a meeting in Hull. I saw someone sitting in the audience. I knew he was an opponent. I said to one of my colleagues, 'You see that fellow over there with a cap over his eyes — we've got to deal with him.' So we went over to him and pulled his cap off, and I said, 'You come out.' I was summoned for assault by this fellow. [*Manny was bound over for six months: his colleague was fined 30 shillings (150p).*]

MacDonald contacted me. He said, 'You must keep out of trouble or you'll damage your career.' I said, 'What am I to do? Allow people to break up my meetings?' And I reminded him about the Charing Cross meeting. I wasn't going to have that. He didn't like it at all.

* * *

He became Prime Minister. He shouldn't have become Prime Minister. We were only a small party, but he accepted it [the premiership]. [We were] the largest single party but still not capable of carrying on for long. Yet he accepted it. I was walking through the lobby, when he was appointing his Cabinet, and I saw him talking to Sir Patrick Hastings. He saw me passing by and said, 'Hey! I want you to go to the Mines Department.' I said, 'I'm not a miner.' He said, 'I want someone impartial, neutral. You go.' I said, 'Am I allowed to consider it?' I had a talk with two of the miners' leaders, Duncan Graham and John Muir, and they said, 'You take the job.'

So I became Secretary for Mines. That's how it was done.

Personal Relations

J.D. "Did you get on with MacDonald personally?"

I'm going to make a confession. No doubt about it, I idolized him for his oratory. He was the great orator of that period [1910–20]. I would put him level with Lloyd George — different in style, but that voice of his — wonderful — a sort of Highland voice, a very refined Scottish accent. There was no sign of Glasgow brogue in it.

When I became an MP [1922], he used to come up to Scotland. On one occasion we brought him to Bathgate, which was part of my constituency. I heard him speak then and he was nothing like as good as when I'd heard him before. He'd started to talk of 'Onward . . . onward and upward . . . ' — rhetoric, meaning nothing at all. He was beginning to fade even at that time.

Now, I must admit I retained friendship with him up to 1931. In 1929 we thought we were going to win. We only lost by a few votes but we hadn't a majority . . . MacDonald wrote to me when I was in my constituency, asking me to get back to London. He was having some trouble about the Cabinet. I didn't know what at the time. I went to Downing Street, and he told me the trouble was the TUC people objected to me being in the government. I said, 'What for?' He said, 'Because a few weeks ago you made a speech in Birmingham on behalf of the ILP, and speaking on industrial democracy, you criticized them [the TUC] in connection with the General Strike [of 1926]. 'But I had to criticize them,' I said, 'because they made such a mess of it. They go into a quarrel, are unprepared for it, and complain about it afterwards [when the strike collapsed]. Look, I'm not going to embarrass you. I'll go to the back benches. I don't care.' I was very independent; very much my style at the time. He said, 'You wait for a while. We'll fix it up somehow.'

I go off to a meeting of the ILP, of which I was a member, with Maxton in the chair . . . When I come in, they ask how I'd got on with Mac — for they'd heard about this business — so I told them what had happened. And they discussed whether I should take a job if offered one. I told them I hadn't decided yet. Maxton was against. He said, 'Come on to the back benches. We'll deal with them.' Incidentally, I'd had a letter from MacDonald criticizing Maxton, because he was afraid Maxton was going to get the leadership of the Labour Party.

Anyway, in 1929 I became Financial Secretary at the War Office. After a while there was trouble with the International Labour Office [a League of Nations creation] about miners' hours of work, and they were considering a possible convention to regulate them in all coal-producing countries. Mac sent for me. Clynes [chairman of the Labour Party] was with him. Mac said to me, 'You've got to leave the War Office. You've got to go to Geneva.' I said, 'Ben Turner [a Labour veteran] is there.' Mac said, 'He won't be able to do the job.' I said, 'I don't want to.' If it hadn't been for Clynes I wouldn't have taken it. I said, 'I've had enough. You told me that because of the TUC I couldn't be in the Cabinet, and now you want me to leave the War Office. I'm getting on quite well.' And so I was. [*Manny said that early experience with the Army greatly helped him in his later successful time at Defence.*]

I went to Geneva. I got a convention — $7\frac{1}{2}$ hours. It never was ratified, as many ILO decisions were not ratified.

Friendship's Decline and Fall

When I was elected in 1922, with a number of Clydesiders and Members from Scotland and South Wales, we held an ILP meeting. [*The Independent Labour Party was an integral and important part of the Labour Party until it disaffiliated from the party in 1936.*] Maxton wanted Wheatley to become leader of the party. I wanted MacDonald, and some wanted Clynes. We didn't come to a decision. A few days later there was a meeting of the Parliamentary Labour Party. Clynes was in the chair. I proposed MacDonald. Maxton proposed Wheatley. I won by five votes.

MacDonald was spectacular — the style — a handsome person, a wonderful speaker at that time. He made a confidant of me. When he went up to live in Frognal, Hampstead, he sent for me. He wasn't very well and he'd say, 'I'm going to resign.' I'd say, 'What a lot of nonsense.'

This was before 1931, when he was PM. He often used to send for me. He'd ask, 'How are the lads getting on? Are they still criticizing me?' He didn't mind criticism from his opponents, but he couldn't take it from his colleagues. He hated it. I used to say, 'They're making their election speeches.' And that would satisfy him for the time being.

Anyway, in 1931 MacDonald decided to form that [National] government. He phoned me and said, 'I want you to remain where you are.' I said, 'I'm sorry, Mac, I've stood by you many times when I didn't understand you. I must stand by the Labour Party.' Only thirteen stood by MacDonald out of the whole Parliamentary Labour Party.

I was out of Parliament for four years. I lost my seat by six hundred votes. There was a communist clique in the constituency: they were trying to get me out. I was in a bad state, financially in a bad state, too. I had £250 a year [salary as overworked nationwide speaker for the party].

I was doing meetings in Durham and Northumberland, and doing very well, becoming very popular. So much so that I was asked to speak at the Durham Miners' Gala, the height of a mark of popularity at the time.

Ebby Edwards, a miners' ex-leader, was Member for Morpeth. He was going to retire and he said, 'You've got the candidature.' It was a safe seat, not as safe as Seaham, but safe. I said, 'All right, Ebby, if you can arrange it — good.' So I was nominally the candidate, but not officially.

And then Seaham asked me to accept nomination. There were another twenty nominations because the Seaham division, against MacDonald, was considered a safe seat, 30,000 majority, as safe as a seat could be. So I went forward, and of all the nominations I topped the poll. So [in 1935] I defeated MacDonald by a majority of 21,000. No one expected that.*

J.D. "Did you ever meet MacDonald again?"
I did see him in the House. He'd never look at me at all. It was ironical: I'd proposed him as leader. I'd defeated him. What could I have done? He'd practically destroyed the Labour Party.

* * *

Though proud of his success at Seaham, I felt that Manny felt sorry that it was necessary. He later reverted to MacDonald, mentioning, but not in a spirit of criticism, his liking for middle-class society. I said I thought it was more a liking for High Society, recalling how I had seen MacDonald being lionized at a gala reception at Londonderry House (my own presence accounted for as reporter for the Yorkshire Post).

---

* *There were then quite distinct Labour and National Labour (MacDonaldite) parties, mutually hostile. MacDonald re-entered the Commons as Member for the since abolished Combined Scottish Universities seat.*

J.D. "MacDonald had a reputation in his later years for being a fearful social snob."
But then we must try and understand the reason for it. Here you are —
a person who had sprung out of nothing — illegitimate — nowadays
that means nothing; in those days it meant something. Ernie Bevin was.
MacDonald came down to London and had to live on 4 shillings (20p) a
week for food. Then he became private secretary to Thomas Lunn, a
Liberal. You've got to take that into account. Somebody like he was —
a fine handsome man, with a capacity for speaking — in those days
oratory counted for something — not like now . . . it's very natural he
should be a bit of a snob.

I often wondered why he was so friendly with me, so confident in confiding in me — whether he thought I had ability and he'd better use it, or
whether there was some other reason.

Iain Macleod

When Macmillan was Prime Minister, a journalist got in touch with me
and said he wanted to talk to me about something connected with the
government. So I met him in Knightsbridge, in a flat. And he told me
that at a dinner at the Dorchester, or one of the hotels, when Tory
ministers were meeting in connection with Africa, Iain Macleod,
although a member of the government, had agreed to something which
was a reversal of the policy he had been advocating in Parliament. [*I
here interpolate, in the interests of clarity, a part of Manny's conversation which in fact occurred later.*]

J.D. "Macleod made his statement on a private occasion?"
Yes, a private occasion, but the point was, it was connected with Kenya.
You may recall there were then two organizations, and one was pretty
much under the control of [Macleod] the Colonial Secretary; the other
was militant and associated with Kenyatta and the Mau-Mau. Now
evidently what Macleod was doing, according to my informant, was that
whilst he had to advocate support for the official party, he actually
supported the militants. It is perfectly true it was a private occasion. I
needn't have done anything about it. If you're told by a responsible
journalist [from the *Yorkshire Post* in this instance], you can either leave
it, or do something about it. I had the feeling that if I didn't do anything
about it [it would come out] later.

I phoned Macleod. I told him, 'I've heard this story.' Know what he said? 'I'd rather not talk about it. You go and see Rab Butler. He'll tell you about it.' So I went to see Rab Butler. I said, 'I've heard about this. I've got to come to some conclusion. I don't want to make a song and dance about it, but I've just got to know.' He said, 'Get in touch with [Lord] Salisbury.' So I wrote to Salisbury. He replied that there was something wrong, but he didn't want to write about it. This seemed to stump me, but I wanted to go a bit further. So I phoned Mac's secretary. I said I wanted to talk to him — something about Macleod. I saw Mac in the Cabinet Room at the Commons. I said, 'I've been told this thing,' and I gave him the details. 'Perhaps Macleod should be warned.' I'd nothing against Macleod. I admired him at the time: he was a very able chap. Mac said, 'Thank you very much for coming. Give me a couple of weeks.' I go. Couple of weeks later, he sends for me. Same room. I sat beside him. 'I've now gone into this, made inquiries,' and he begins to explain what happened. I listened to his explanation. I knew at once it was no explanation at all: he had to get out of it somehow. He wasn't going to bring Macleod back into the picture, because a question might have been asked in Parliament and Macleod might have been in trouble. So after Mac stopped talking, after about ten minutes, I said, 'Prime Minister, I've only got two answers. The first is I cannot accept your explanation. Second, I'm going to take no further action.' He turned to me and thanked me. I stood up to go out. He put his arm round my shoulder. He said, 'You're a decent fellow.'

Personal History

You Need To Be Tough

Having regard to my early upbringing — when I think how I got through, made a name for myself — I wonder how I did it.

I've got [a tough constitution]. When involved with seamen, often someone offered to fight me. Mostly I'd say, 'Oh, no.' Discretion was the better part of valour. Not that I was afraid. I needn't have been because I was pretty good with my fists. I exercised with dumb-bells, weight-lifting, that sort of thing. I punched the ball every morning until I was fifty. No wonder that when I hit that fellow in Glasgow, in order to defend MacDonald, he had to go to the Infirmary. I had a tremendous punch in those days.

Harold Macmillan

The best of the Tory crowd — except for Churchill in wartime — was Harold Macmillan. No question about it — shrewd, astute . . . I recall when he came into Parliament: he was a Fabian, pursued the middle way, supported the creation of public utility corporations. He was half-Socialist. Some years later when I was Member for Seaham, he was standing for Stockton.

I went down on the eve of the poll and I made it impossible for him to win. I was very popular then. I probably didn't deserve it, but I was. I'd defeated MacDonald — that helped. The audience was crowded — up the walls. What was I to do about Macmillan?

I said — as I sometimes do when I'm speaking — something no one expects. I said I remembered reading something American and I came across a word I couldn't understand. I'll tell you what it was; it was 'Mugwump'.*

'And what do you think it means?' I asked. 'It means a man who sits on the fence with his mug on one side and his wump on the other. That's Macmillan.' The place roared with laughter. Next thing, it was all over the place, 'Mugwump'. Macmillan also claimed afterwards that that caused his defeat. He had to go down to Bromley [Kent]. He's a great man.

Mac's Helping Hand

I wanted some official reports, when I was writing one of my books, and I asked the Ministry of Fuel and Power to let me have them. The civil servants wouldn't agree [again] — Official Secrets Act — 30-year rule . . . So I couldn't get them. [See COAL.] I waited some time and then I determined I was going to get them. By that time Macmillan had become Prime Minister, so I phoned and asked if I could see him. Yes, he said. I told him, 'They won't let me see the reports. What's the Secrets Act got to do with it? There's no security question.' He agreed. He gave me a room in the Cabinet Office, with a key, to use myself.

See MACLEOD.

* N. American Indian origin, meaning Chief, and thus no insult. Later applied to a political independent. Pejorative usage more modern.

Monarchy

J.D. "Obviously you would approve a continuation of the monarchical system, unlike some members of your old party. There is quite a lot of republicanism in the party, isn't there?"

There is. The only way I can deal with your question is to refer to the occasion in the House of Lords when I was asked, most unusually for someone who was an ex-Minister, to move the motion of the Address to Her Majesty. I wondered why I was asked. Anyhow, I decided I would do what I always do — speak without notes . . . The line I took was this: about presidents — I've experience of presidents in various parts of the world, they were always getting into trouble of some kind. We are able to carry on quite constitutionally . . . And then I referred to the Social Contract, which was being talked about, and pointed out that the feeling is strong but the flesh is weak — the difficulty of the TUC in giving a guarantee that can be carried out. You have a president — you have all these difficulties . . . why bother about a president? I did it in that form, which was taken very well by the House. It was unusual for me to be asked to do it, but even more unusual to do it without a note. No one had ever done that before – or has since.

J.D. "Republicanism — which is mostly unspoken except by Willie Hamilton — seems to be latent in the left of the Labour party. You can't be a marxist and support a monarchical system, can you?"

It doesn't bother me very much.

J.D. "I'm thinking of its effect on the electorate."

Nor do I think it bothers them. If ever the country is in difficulties they'll rally around, and the monarchy is the central feature which encourages them. They may be critical of it . . . but they don't have any feeling of malice or disappointment about the monarchy. And as far as I'm concerned. . . if I were asked frankly — and no one can accuse me of being too right-wing — if I were asked to vote between appointment of a president or retaining the existing monarchy, I would vote for monarchy. We avoid constitutional difficulties. The monarch doesn't interfere in legislation — or doesn't appear to do so. Therefore, as far as I'm concerned, as long as this country wants a monarchy it can have it. But I can understand that in the course of time there may be changes as in the past when members of the monarchy have misbehaved. While that could be tolerated in the seventeenth or eighteenth centuries, it might not be tolerated in the twenty-first century.

J.D. "It wasn't tolerated in the twentieth century — Edward VIII."

The country accepted King George VI. I didn't have much experience of King Edward. He went down to meet the miners, but I had little experience of him. I met George VI, whom I liked very much. I remember my wife and I attending Buckingham Palace; my wife offered the King a cigarette and amused him by saying it came from Scotland. When the Queen was a Princess, I found her very friendly — and particularly the Queen Mother, very friendly indeed. Even Queen Mary. I remember when I was a member of the government and was introduced to her in the royal pavilion at a Garden Party at Buckingham Palace, and she said to someone, 'So that's him, is it!'

Field Marshal Viscount Montgomery

It's extraordinary — people have referred [with surprise] to the fact that I was friendly with Monty, got on so well. It was so easy. There was never friction of any kind. He used to say the most amazing things. When he became an international soldier, he never came to London without visiting me at the Ministry of Defence. He talked about things, and if they were bad he'd say, 'You and I have got to start a revolution!' He would criticize everybody but me. Do you know what he suggested before the 1951 election, when we were defeated? He said, 'You've got to stay.' I said 'I don't know about that. I think we're going to lose.' He said, 'It doesn't matter about that. You've got to stay. I'll fix it with Churchill.' As sure as I'm here, that's what he said!

* * *

I would say — dealing as Minister and Chief of Imperial General Staff — the most remarkable thing about him was that he hardly ever mentioned a general on his staff without saying he was first-class. Would you believe that?

J.D. "Yes, because he'd have got rid of any that weren't."
[*Manny ignored this.*] Suppose we discovered a certain general was a homosexual. And that becomes known to Monty through the discovery of a diary. And it's brought to me as Minister to decide. What do we do?

79

Expose him? No. As a matter of fact, that general became associated with the United Nations, occupying a very important post. What did we do? I said he |Monty| had to consider the effect on the Army. Monty said, 'Precisely! It's not what WE feel about him — it's the repercussions.'

* * *

We never had a quarrel. He quarrelled with all sorts of people, never with me. Sometimes people tend to indicate |that| I did what he told me. Quite the opposite. He had troubles with the previous minister |A.B.| Alexander . . . There was trouble the whole time. He |Monty| admits he threatened the government: he would expose what happened in Palestine unless they did certain things. I came to the conclusion — if I'm going to meet Monty and the same thing happens, I'm finished. Perhaps that what my colleagues wanted. I doubted their loyalty.

* * *

|Monty| came to the House of Commons |when Deputy Supremo of NATO| to listen to a debate, and he wrote to me about it. In the letter, he asked, 'Who was that barmy bloke attacking me?' You know who he meant? Denis Healey, Minister of Defence at the time.

See DRINKING.

Miscellany

The items in this section, mostly brief, are in the nature of 'asides' — comments on people and things which came into conversations that were not primarily concerned with them. As do we all, even if we mean not to, Manny would frequently digress as memory prompted him temporarily to desert the mainstream of thought or reminiscence.

Lord Beaverbrook
He was very interested in me for a while.

J.D. "Did you like him?"
Well, I always had this feeling: is he trying to use me? I'll say this,

despite the criticism of Beaverbrook, I never disliked him. I remember one night during the war at a dinner Hannen Swaffer [the Socialist journalist] was there and I was talking about the shipping business, my subject. I was telling Beaverbrook about the convoy system, which I objected to. I wanted ships built with proper speed. Anyway, Swaffer later said to me, 'The Beaver wasn't in form tonight.' I do understand from statements made to me by people associated with Express News-papers, that sometime [after that wartime meeting] he gave instructions: no criticism of Shinwell.

Aneurin Bevan
Bevan was a great debater — but he could be very nasty.

Ernest Bevin
All sorts of things have been said about him. He was quite different to what people thought he was.

* * *

Ernie Bevin was a great character . . . He was all right so long as you agreed with him. It didn't matter what the subject was: if you agreed with him, it was all right. If you disagreed with him, you were the enemy. When I became Minister for Defence, he [as Foreign Secretary] said to me, 'You and I have got to work together.' It was the first time he ever said that. Years before, we were fighting each other all the time. I didn't like him over the Palestine business. [Bevin tended to be pro-Arab.]

Lord (Bob) Boothby
He could easily have been Prime Minister. He had the ability. I've told him to his face, 'Why you failed, Bob, is you loved love more than you loved life.'

British Character
What's remarkable about the British character is its ability to adapt and recover from recurrent crises.

This is departing from the somewhat pessimistic line I've been inclined to develop. I would say there is nothing in the sphere of individual or social well-being which is beyond OUR capacity. The number of able people that we have in the United Kingdom . . . for the most part they work along individual lines. We don't fully use them, don't fully use our resources, all our resources.

81

Personal History

A Close Shave With Death

After a period of unemployment, I got a job with the Scottish Co-operative Society . . . and a two-room flat in the Fairfield district [of Glasgow]. There I joined the local branch of the ILP and engaged in most of its propaganda activities. My work in the Co-operative factory was dull. What made matters worse was my disappointment with the Co-operative Movement. I failed to understand why those employed were no better off than those in private firms. No doubt conditions have vastly improved. The manager of the factory where I worked was an ignorant bully.

The opportunity to escape came at the beginning of 1911. My wages in the Co-op job were 35/- a week (175p), hardly enough to keep a wife and two children in comfort. We lived frugally. I did smoke — a pipe only — the tobacco was usually supplied by seamen for services rendered. My work for seamen came about this way: Havelock Wilson, the seamen's leader, had called a strike of seamen and asked Glasgow Trades Council [*of which Manny was a prominent member*] for support. I offered my services. Already men had left their ships. Wilson was associated with the Labour movement as far back as the '80s and became MP for Middlesbrough. [He was subsequently expelled from the party.] His National Union of Seamen was always in financial trouble . . . there were rumours about improper use of funds. However, although aware of Wilson's reputation, we agreed to assist the seamen because of their shocking wages and working conditions. I took part in negotiations with the shipowners and we were able to obtain an assurance that the deck-hands and stockhold men would receive what they asked for.

Unfortunately, we learned that Wilson had reached an agreement with the Shipping Federation to accept reduced increases [with the proviso that Wilson's union would have a monopoly for jobs]. Wilson sent two of his colleagues [one later exposed as a rogue] to the Clyde to close our branch because we had obtained a higher rate.

My experiences during that period were more than exciting. I was threatened by thugs, and on one occasion was fired at by one of Wilson's men, with the result that the man standing next to me was killed. The culprit was acquitted on the grounds of self-defence!

Communism

J.D. "Going back to your early days, when you were just getting interested in politics, seeking the meaning of socialism, you must have been attracted, like many young people, to the idea of communism."

No, never — strangely. Because of what was happening in Russia. Had Lenin lived, and done what I think he wanted to do, I think I might have inclined that way. What I couldn't stand were the purges, the blood-baths. I couldn't understand them killing each other. These were the fellows I'd heard about, read about, some of them I'd met in Geneva when I'd gone there on behalf of the government . . . when I thought of them being bumped off by their own colleagues! And the Trotsky business. Trotsky to me was a hero.

I remember when the communist party was founded in London — but I wouldn't have anything to do with it at all. Then I was regarded as being on the Left, when I was in fact, occasionally, very much on the Right.

Willie Gallacher

One-time leader of the British Communist party:

Willie was a communist, but you'd never believe he was. He was a wonderful person. I was in prison with him. He only got three months — but I got five!

Conferences

There's a Labour Party Conference, there's a Liberal one, an SDP, a Conservative . . . And they all talk their heads off. ALL they do is talk and talk. It's not very satisfactory: the problems remain.

J.D. "All conferences are held for the benefit of those attending them."

Richard Crossman

Referring to the Bruce Lockhart memoirs, of which he had been critical in one instance:

I tell you what did please me was when he said something about Crossman, something nasty about Crossman. That always pleases me — because if I was right about anything I was right about him. Crossman regarded everybody as inferior.

Fatalism

I don't believe, considering all these factors [*after a rambling conversation covering various 'problems'*] that one CAN find a satisfactory solution — any more than one can find a solution to ANY problem. We talk and talk, and we're baffled . . . We talk [in the Lords] and there's no implementation of ideas.

J.D. "Did anyone ever solve anything?"
We're on to philosophy. Has anyone ever solved anything? NO!

Michael Foot

The idea that Michael Foot could have taken us [Labour] out of any kind of crisis was such a mistake, such a blunder, such an error of judgement. Michael Foot — a decent person — liberal-minded, brought up in the Liberal movement — his father was a great liberal — moderate in character — all his brothers are liberal in character — great journalist, a great fighter. But no more than that. Judgement? He changed his mind over and over again, on defence and other matters.

* * *

He was a good speaker; not now. His style of speaking is outmoded. He was a first-class journalist; as a leader, no. As an agitator, yes. He was associated with most of the rebellions [in the Labour ranks]. If he didn't do the job himself, he would inspire somebody else.

J.D. "The word demagogue comes to mind."
The word is offensive . . .

J.D. "It's meant to be!"
. . . one doesn't want to be offensive to Foot. One's got a certain sympathy for him.

(Lord) George-Brown

Now he's a businessman. He just pops into the Lords for a minute — and out he goes. He treats the Lords with contempt — as he does many people. For some time I never bothered with him. I quarrelled with him over the Middle East, violently, in the House of Commons, and I made no bones about it. Over the Common Market, I was the very opposite to him in my opinions. We fought on that. Well, then he left the Labour Party, and I would not even nod to him. But then he would come and speak to me and I let it [our disagreements] pass. And that's the extent of our relationship.

I've often said this, and I've told him myself: he's got a lot of talent and he's misused it. As a result, he failed to become what he wanted — leader of the Labour Party and Prime Minister. The reason why a few of us organized to achieve success for Harold Wilson was not that we were enthusiastic about Wilson, but because we couldn't tolerate Brown. The opposition to Brown was organized by [the late Lord] Wigg and myself, when there was a good deal of whisperings and innuendo about Wilson's personal behaviour. We fought it in the tea-rooms and smoke-rooms and we made certain Brown would not get in [as leader]. Brown had a good deal of personal support: I remember quarrelling with some of those, who were prominent Ministers at the time — most of them [now] dead. I wouldn't have Brown at any price, wouldn't trust him. And I think we were right about that. He would never have made a good leader — too erratic and unreliable. Wilson — he could be relied on.

Sometimes I see him [George-Brown] when we are leaving the House. I'm getting into my minicab, and his car comes along with a chauffeur. I laugh at it all: it's all great fun. He's made a lot of money: he needed to make it. I asked John Junor [editor of the *Sunday Express*], 'Why do you employ Brown?' 'Because he's available: there's no other reason,' he says.

Denis Healey
Despite what Healey says, he doesn't see what's happening. Trouble with Healey is that he's had too much experience, in the wrong places — Chancellor of the Exchequer and Defence Secretary.

Personal History

A Success for the Disadvantaged

When the war ended in 1918, Lloyd George decided to form a coalition government. I stood [at Linlithgow/West Lothian] for the first time in that election [1919] and gained a considerable Labour vote, the highest in any County division in Scotland. But I was defeated. I had no trade union backing, hardly any money, one old broken-down car — but many friends.

I remained a candidate for that constituency and devoted attention to it. It came to my knowledge that men and women who worked in the Glasgow Asylum for the Blind, themselves sightless, were being treated in a fashion one would not expect to exist in what was a charitable institution. It was alleged the manager was a tyrant, that conditions as regards payment, hours of labour and social needs of those blind people were not brought to the notice of either the public or even subscribers to the institution.

A delegation of three of these blind people approached me and asked if I would help. I am reluctant to enter into any quarrel or any activity suggested to me, but once convinced that action is required because of the moral principle involved, my hesitation disappears. If I am to take part, I must do it with all the intensity in my possession. I can't tolerate anything that appears unjust.

So I waited until the next Annual Meeting [having become a subscriber to the charity], by which time I had organized something of an opposition. I obtained the support of a well-known lawyer with radical sympathies. We had the familiar proceedings . . . a short optimistic speech from the chair . . . statement of accounts . . . usual applause from subscribers . . .

Then we struck, demanding that complaints from some of the sightless should be heard. There was a terrific rumpus, almost a scuffle, which led to police intervention. At first sight, this would have seemed to be complete defeat for us — but the newspapers the next day gave a full report. I had the satisfaction of learning, not long afterwards, that wages and conditions had improved, and the sightless people were overjoyed that the tyranny to which they had been subjected had been removed.

If I cannot claim any other achievement, this will suffice.

Importance of History

In order to understand the existing situation, one must have some historical knowledge, delve into the past. Without that one can't possibly come to a reasonable conclusion, be rational. How true it is that few people do have knowledge of past events. Let me give you an example, without going into politics but referring to politicians. This is not imaginary: it's what occurred.

I recall sitting in the House of Commons, in the tea-room with colleagues, MPs, younger than me — if not in years, in experience and length of service. We were talking about some pioneers of the Labour movement and I happened to mention Tom Mann. One asked 'Who's Tom Mann?' I said, 'Never heard of Tom Mann?' Several said they hadn't. I had to tell them — one of our greatest orators, a founder of the Independent Labour Party, a man who went to prison for his opinions, who was perhaps the most electrifying speaker we ever had. That's one illustration. I doubt whether 25 per cent of MPs — on one side or the other — have fully seized the [importance of] past historical events. Maybe some who'd gone to universities, read history — but I doubt whether they've tried to understand it in relation to existing conditions.

I was in the House of Lords [a year or so ago], when what's called the 'recession' had started. I happened to say, 'Oh, well, we've had it all before.' And somebody, who's been a member of a Conservative Cabinet — I won't give his name, no point — a university man at the highest level — he said, 'Rubbish — you're talking rubbish — never had it like this before.' And I said, 'And you've read history!' He dismissed me, just like that, [snap of fingers.] I thought a lot about that.

Manny, a long-time student of history — great admiration for George Macaulay Trevelyan, OM — went on to comment on the series of 'recessions' from the Industrial Revolution onwards.

James Maxton
The once celebrated, much caricatured, ILP MP:

Great orator, but apart from his oratory — nothing else. He would never accept a job or anything of that sort. He wouldn't get up until twelve o'clock in the morning. He was indolent: that was his trouble. He became chairman of the Independent Labour Party for a while, when I was chairman of its administrative council. MacDonald couldn't stand Maxton. MacDonald always considered Maxton a kind of rival, because of his oratory. But Maxton never wanted the job — except to be allowed to speak. He was a school teacher, and a Conservative, to start with. When he was at Glasgow university, he was a Conservative.

J.D. "He was very popular as a personality, even with Conservatives."
In the House of Commons he was very popular — no question. But he had his weaknesses, and if he couldn't get his own way he would dissolve into tears. Curious that way . . . he never bothered about anything. He could have been leader [of Labour]. He preferred to be leader of the ILP than be second fiddle . . . He looked like a pirate.

Middle-class Revolutionaries?
I would go so far as to say that the changes that are likely in the next twenty-five to forty years will be brought about — suggested and perhaps implemented — by the so-called middle class. By middle class, I mean the type associated with the Civil Service — not the middle class people who have mansions in the country and all that, but the true middle class [amongst whom Manny had elsewhere placed such contrasting persons as Mrs Thatcher and Tony Benn.]

I believe it's much more likely that if any big change — even revolutionary change — occurs, it will be effected through the middle class rather than the working class.

Of course, middle-class revolutionaries are at least as old as the French Revolution and, according to Paul Johnson, as modern as today.

He wrote in the Spectator *that he considered the* Daily Mirror *had been 'wrecked by middle-class revolutionaries'.*

Nationality
I'm in favour of a child born in this country being considered a British citizen. There were a lot of legal people talking [about it in the Lords] with a forensic ability I don't possess — and I said so. But I said this wasn't a forensic matter: if a child was born in this country, which is quite accidental, it must be British.

Politicians
We need more statesmen and fewer politicians. Because when one considers what Parliamentarians DO . . . they're concerned with their own careers, their salaries and expenses, and thinking about the next election. That applies not only to the rank and file but to the leaders.

Presidents
The only President I respect was Truman. Jack Kennedy? I got the impression that had he lived sooner or later he would have destroyed himself with his *affaires*.

Arthur Scargill
J.D. *"Scargill's the very sort of person who frightens the moderate Socialist voter."*
Don't forget, even the Callaghan government got in with a large majority — and the Scargill crowd were as active as can be then.

J.D. *"I don't think he came quite to the general public's attention as he has later."*
But don't forget — THEY are at it all the time . . . the communists in the unions, the Labour Party. We know who they are.

Peter Shore
Shore has got everything but the one thing that's necessary as a leader — to be spectacular. You see, you can have all the ability in the world, the intelligence, but unless you can get it across, it's not much use. Sometimes that's more important than anything else. That and behaviour. Behaviour is very important.

United Nations
We formed [after World War One] the League of Nations, only to discover it was a myth. So we formed the United Nations — which is a

shambles. If it was abolished tomorrow, it wouldn't make the slightest difference — in fact, things might improve as a result.

Isaac (Lord) Wolfson

Answering a question, Manny said he was no longer much of a contributor to Jewish charities, preferring more personal forms of benevolence. He said he still had several old constituents to whom he sent presents of money. I asked if he had had contact with such well-known philanthropists as Lord Wolfson who has given so much to Israel.

I met Isaac Wolfson on the *Queen Mary* when I came across [from official meetings in the USA in 1950]. He stopped me, and immediately started talking politics. I said, 'You know all about business and I don't know a damned thing about it. I know all about politics, and you don't know a damned thing about them.' That's the only conversation I've had with him.

My first wife knew the family well — very friendly with the Wolfsons when they were just ordinary people, traders — long before there was any question of wealth — and probably if she hadn't married me she'd have married one of them, and become a millionairess. I think she was happier with me! I hope so. They were very well known in the Gorbals district of Glasgow. In those days they were hawkers — they used to go out into the Highlands, to the farmers, with a pack on their backs, selling all sorts of odds and ends. And so they built up their fortunes.

Personal History

Strong Arm of the Law: Arrest

In 1919, the Clyde Workers' Committee approached the Glasgow Trades Council, of which I was president, to help secure a reduction in hours of labour, in order to absorb the unemployed. The Trades Council decided two members should meet the Clyde Workers' Committee. I was one of those selected. The question arose of forming a committee to organize demonstrations. I was proposed as chairman. Because of the unanimous demand, I reluctantly agreed. We held meetings in various parts of Glasgow and in neighbouring towns. Prominent members of the Labour Party rendered assistance. The official unions were opposed to us.

After a series of demonstrations that got us nowhere, it was decided one should be organized in George Square, Glasgow, in the city centre, and a delegation should interview the Lord Provost and ask him to intercede with the Prime Minister. I was a member of the Town Council and had access to the City Chambers. The demonstration practically filled the square: probably 80,000 people were there. Among my colleagues were David Kirkwood, also a Town Councillor, and William Gallacher [the communist]. No speeches were made. It was decided Kirkwood and myself should enter the municipal buildings, leaving Gallacher with strict instructions to maintain order.

The Lord Provost was disinclined even to listen to us. Meanwhile, it appeared that a tramcar was making its way through the square, to the annoyance of some demonstrators. There was something of a scuffle. Unable to get anything useful from the Lord Provost, Kirkwood and I left. By this time hundreds of police were in sight and began using their batons in brutal fashion. Unfortunately, some of the crowd were forced up a side street, where there happened to be a lorry stacked with bottles, which they began to hurl at the police.

During my public life, I have seldom been critical of the police . . . in my experience they have proved their worth. But the action of some during the demonstration in George Square was deplorable. Within a few minutes, the Sheriff appeared and read the Riot Act. When I left the Chambers, the police had succeeded in dividing the crowd, so I stood on a seat and tried to persuade people to leave the square. . . .

About one-thirty in the morning there was a knock on my door. Several policemen came in. One said, 'We have come to arrest you.'

Nationalization

After many years of struggle and strife and propaganda and expenditure, a government comes into power with a huge majority — the Attlee government [of 1945] — and I can speak with some authority because I was a member of that government, occupying three positions: Power, War and Defence . . .

We produced a Socialist programme; nationalization of the Bank of England, most of the mining industry, electricity, gas, part of the transport industry, civil aviation. That's going a long way in the direction of Socialism. Now, that was done, and for a while the country accepted it. And then that [acceptance] vanished because it [Socialism] wasn't effective, didn't work somehow. When I say 'didn't work', it wasn't beneficial in the sense of our problems disappearing — the problem of unemployment, financial problems, trading problems and various international problems. It didn't produce peace in the world and so on and so forth . . .

A government comes to power after many years of strife and it produces a Socialist policy. And after a few years, another government comes in and destroys it. Not only do they destroy it but create such devastation, disorganization, that it's almost impossible to revive it.

J.D. "There was no de-nationalization of parts of the economy you've mentioned — power, etc . . ."
Look at the situation: not a single one of them is viable. There's not much value in a policy [being] put into operation if isn't viable. Surely, the whole purpose of change in some organizations is that what emerges should be viable.

J.D. "It isn't any change in government that renders them non-viable. When the Conservatives came back, they left coal and steel and gas still nationalized."
What is likely to emerge is possibly some new method of organizing and administrating primary industries — and it may not be along the lines of public ownership. That's how it seems to be working out.

J.D. "Take the case of British Leyland: it seems to have the worst of both worlds. It isn't formally nationalized, but on the other hand it's not an independent company . . ."
It depends completely on finance furnished by the taxpayer.

J.D. "Does the State go on supplying it for ever? It's got to go on supporting coal and steel for ever."
May we not reach a point where the electors will not bear the cost of industries — however important they might be for the nation or the people employed — where the industry depends on subsidies? We know there are countries whose industries couldn't exist without subsidies — railways are universally subsidised, and so is shipping — but I don't believe the electors will bear that [indefinitely].

Steel Mistake?

I was against steel nationalization. It's such a wide-ranging industry. They nationalized the production of steel. I was against it on the grounds that one had to consider the effect on other industries. I opposed it very strongly, and they were angry with me, particularly Ernie Bevin — furious with me because of that.

But I was right.

How To De-nationalize

If I had to deal with public ownership NOW, I wouldn't bother about the Cripps method. He wanted an Enabling Bill, so you could nationalize when you liked. He was off his head at the time.

Take an industry: the time has come when it has to be organized by some corporate [State] body in the interests of the country and of the industry itself and those employed in it. Talk the whole thing over — with the workers as well. I wouldn't nationalize as we — the Attlee government — did. Don't forget: the mines, civil aviation, ports partly, steel — whose nationalization I opposed — all went through.

J.D. "There's a Fabian element in what you say — the inevitability of gradualness: a pretty meaningless phrase — not trying to force things too fast".
Take coal: we should have nationalized it WHOLLY — processing, distribution, the whole thing, so it became a permanent feature of daily life. Very difficult to upset it then.

J.D. "How could one de-nationalize coal? Who'd want to buy it?"
Blimey! You don't buy the whole lot. You carve it up.

J.D. "Sell individual mines?"
No, no — you go back to districts. You take mines in a particular part of the country which are thriving, and you process the coal in that area. In another area, which isn't so prosperous, you're very careful. Close pits down if you think them unnecessary. There are many parts of the country where mines are in production which thirty years ago would have been closed.

Manny had forgotten de-nationalization: efficient nationalization was his goal.

Capitalism Conditionally Acceptable

I referred to our 'semi-nationalization' where the State holds anything from a controlling interest to minority of shares in major companies.

It's a form of nationalization. When I was touring the country for the

Labour party [1923–5], when talking about nationalization I would often say this — and I was much criticized for it by colleagues: 'I am not concerned about nationalization [for its own sake]. If a company owned by shareholders runs its business, with a vast number of employees, and ensures regular employment, good wages, and good conditions — and satisfies consumers — then I don't want nationalization.' I said that over and over again. Then I will accept capitalism; as long as direction of [basic industrial] policy rests with the government of the day.

J.D. "Would you recommend the nationalization of the insurance industry, the banks?"
Possibly insurance . . . As regards the banks, I would hesitate to interfere with them. As long as they have consideration for the national interest. That is watched over by the Bank of England. I think it works very well. I don't see the sense of nationalizing something if it's working all right.

J.D. "That is where you differ from some in your party who would nationalize for the sake of nationalizing, without practical considerations."
It becomes a principle. It's a fixed idea. You want to abolish capitalism: why take over the banks unless you're sure you can operate them satisfactorily? Better leave them as they are.

Personal History

Strong Arm of the Law: Imprisonment

[Following the George Square demo and arrest at home] I was taken to the local police station and placed in a cell with no furniture of any kind. So I lay on the floor and went to sleep: I was tired out. The only person who spoke to me was a detective who said, 'You will get five years for this.' I asked him, for what? 'For rioting,' he said. I almost laughed.

* * *

Why was it that the Sheriff appeared so readily? Why were hundreds of police available within seconds of the tramcar incident? If there was any incitement or intention to riot, why was no evidence to that effect given at our trial in Edinburgh? Incitement to riot was certainly never the purpose of the demonstrators, myself or others. We later learned that a member of the government told the Prime Minister that he thought the demonstration was intended to start a revolution. It was only eighteen months after the Revolution in Russia. What happened in George Square — the presence of police, tanks in the streets and soldiers on rooftops — was a deliberate act on the part of Lloyd George.

* * *

Not only was there an absence of evidence at the Court of Sessions to justify accusations of rioting or incitement to riot, but the presiding judge acquitted ten of the twelve accused, and expressed doubts about any threat of revolution by sending Gallacher to prison for only three months and myself for five months — perhaps because I was chairman of the committee.

I was sent to Calton gaol in Edinburgh, one of the most squalid prisons in the country. I expected to be treated as a political prisoner but, said the ex-military governor, 'there's no such thing in Scotland.' The food was abominable. From the prison doctor and governor my treatment was most objectionable. By the chief warder and his colleagues I was treated with the utmost consideration. No privileges, of course: I practically lived on the horrible porridge, and bread, throughout my sentence. I must admit I was much healthier on my release than on my entry!

Northern Ireland

J.D. "I'm sure you are not going to say you have a solution — like most politicians do. Have you any suggestions as to how we might solve the Ulster problem?"

I became acquainted with South and North Ireland — the Irish people — many years ago, and I conceived an affection for both. I found the Irish are a lovable people. I knew about the rebels: I knew many of them when I lived in Scotland. I came to know more of them when I became associated with the seafaring community, in which many were involved. I also got to know the Orange Order in Northern Ireland — and found them quite different in private to what they seemed in public. I used to visit Northern Ireland on holiday or on seamen's business. I haven't any feelings of bitterness, but I can't stand people being shot in the back. I can tolerate war somehow — that's fighting an enemy — retaliation — but terrorism, shooting unnecessarily — murder — that's something I can't stand at all.

After considerable talking around the subject:

. . . A united Ireland eventually — I'm aware that's politically |now| unacceptable. That's the eventual solution. One day |the two parts of the country| will be merged.

J.D. "Would a re-drawing of the borders help, at the moment? They are manifestly absurd."

I'm not so sure that's the solution. Geographically it would appear to be so. I venture this opinion — and I do so because it impinges on a subject I often seek to avoid: theology. Having read Irish history, a great deal of it, in my opinion the trouble in Ireland is of a |religious| sectarian character. It's partly economic, but primarily sectarian. And not until the sectarian differences are resolved will it be possible to create a united Ireland. When the Protestants and Catholics settle their sectarian differences and realize they are human beings, and if they believe in the Almighty and have allegiance to Him, when that happens the Irish problem will be easily removed.

J.D. "But there's no sectarianism in the South, despite the considerable Protestant population there who live in perfect amity with their neighbours."

Whether it's Ireland, or Scotland, England, India or Africa, the problems are not the problems that exist between ordinary people, but the problems between their so-called leaders. If we could persuade the leaders to be a bit more open-minded . . .

The problem of Northern Ireland will not be removed until certain people disappear.

Parliament

I posed the proposition that the broadcasting of Parliamentary proceedings — with special reference to the House of Commons — was a mistake and 'has done enormous harm to the system'.

The demand for broadcasting came very largely from the public themselves. They wanted to hear what MPs were saying. I never was very enthusiastic about it, because I always felt, as a Member, that often one was looking up to the |Press| gallery to see if one's views were accepted. That won't do. Again, it's a matter of independence. You express your own opinions: you don't care whether the gallery likes it or not . . .

I return to a point I've often made. What an MP wants is to be mentioned — doesn't care how much the Press criticizes him, attacks him — can be devastating — but 'For heaven's sake, mention me! That's the one thing I want!' Just like an actor or a footballer — worst thing that can happen to him is not to be mentioned.

The Commons "Bear Garden"

J.D. "I was referring to the bear-garden atmosphere that comes over so often on radio broadcasts from the House of Commons — in contrast to the Lords — where you get this frightful shouting and 'sit down' and 'shut up' coming over the air. It really sounds as if these people were at breaking-up day at a school. It creates a frightful impression on the public."

I would agree with that. I think that this bickering that goes on, the abuse . . .

J.D. "The howling down of the Prime Minister or the Leader of the Opposition — they can hardly get their answers over sometimes."

I've witnessed scenes in the House of Commons that were ghastly. I recall the situation over Suez . . . I never heard anything like it. And the curious thing about it was the people making the most noise, indulging in the most abusive expressions, almost ready to use their fists, were — who do you think? The pacifists! I can see them now. As a matter of fact there is one of them in the House of Lords — I'd rather not mention his name.

J.D. "Why not?"

He might not like it! I can remember hearing him shouting his head off, saying terrible things over Suez. He went on for several months, as many of them did. Nearly all pacifists, furious about this — this idea that France and Israel and Britain joining together to fight the poor

Egyptians was a terrible thing! They [the pacifists] had not thought at all about the action taken by Nasser, the effect of that on the Middle East, on the Suez Canal and on international trade . . .

Blame Members, Not Radio

J.D. *"In those days, this [Parliamentary uproar] was only reported in writing. But now people are hearing this almost childish behaviour from their elected representatives."*
Don't forget this: events such as I've described take place — but are immediately followed by an event even more ghastly, more shocking! So it's forgotten.

J.D. *"I'm not talking about what's actually said. The behaviour in the House is so appalling on many occasions . . . if it wasn't broadcast it wouldn't matter — if one just read about it."*
Surely you would agree that if it's done, it's just as well the public should hear it? [*I persist in my opinion that the whole Parliamentary system is being brought into disrepute.*]

It seems to me that if that's the kind of people they are, if they misbehave in that fashion, it's as well for their constitutents to hear it. What brings Parliament into contempt is not the broadcasting, but the behaviour.

If there's a sense of injustice, tempers can flare — no doubt about it — but it can go too far. [*Manny strongly implied that the Speaker should sometimes exert firmer discipline.*] What you've said is absolutely right: you should never howl a Minister down. Always listen to what your opponent says. I dislike this preventing someone from speaking. If you want freedom of expression for yourself, you must want it for others. I would regard it, as a debater, as very important to listen to the other person's point of view. [*Manny blamed some of the bad temper and poor manners displayed in the Commons on the Parliamentary time-table and long hours put in by some Members.*]

If Parliament could undertake it's functions in a rational fashion, starting at a proper time and ending at a proper time, it might be different.

* * *

Excessive Loyalty to Parties

It does seem to me that what is more likely to happen than anything else is a situation where MPs — though associated with a political party — must become more and more independent. One of the dangers to which we are subjected is the demanding of excessive loyalty from members of a party once they have joined it. That idea would [become] completely outmoded. The public, the electors, will be much more likely to support MPs in the coming years who are independent, who express personal views whilst accepting principles associated with their political parties. That's quite the opposite to what a section of the Labour Party have decided.

* * *

Isn't it possible that people will get tired of these political parties? . . . It could well be that this new organization, which is only in its infancy [the Liberal–SDP Alliance] might represent a much more effective political opinion in this country than any other.

This shows Manny's acceptance of all possibilities: mainly he was dismissive of the Alliance as a practicable Parliamentary alternative, as opposed to a theoretical one.

It's amazing that if anyone has to say twenty or thirty words, they have to read it out. I've never read a speech for over forty years. Fewer of them now read speeches as a result of my laughing at them. It's supposed to be out of order. Occasionally a Member points out that another is reading — but the Speaker takes no notice.

The "Shinwell High Tea"

In the House of Commons, when I went there first — when there was an upsurge of Labour supporters in '22 — one could go into the dining-room and have a dinner for 3s 6d ($17\frac{1}{2}$p), and quite a good dinner, and there was a regular tip of 6d ($2\frac{1}{2}$p). Quite a number of the Labour Members couldn't afford three-and-six: salaries were very low and no expenses. Well, they came to me, the Yorkshire and Durham Members . . . to say what they wanted was 'high tea'. We don't want the dinner. Get us 'high tea'. We're accustomed to that. I said, 'You want a bit of bacon and egg, a bit of fish, a roll and butter, a pot of tea. We'll see if we can get that.' 'We can't afford more than about 1s 6d ($7\frac{1}{2}$p),' they said. I said I'd see the manager. He didn't like the idea: 'The waiters won't like it — to serve specially this sort of thing.' I had a discussion — I think with one of the secretaries of the railway unions — and he promised to come and help me with the manager. So we both saw him and we persuaded him to try it. He said we could take a corner of the restaurant, with a couple of tables, for eight people altogether, and he would try to get some of the waiters to serve them. So we decided to go ahead, and then we had to consider the tip, because, as I say, the tip was 6d. We decided on 3d. We used to be looked on as inferior people. I'd helped them so I had to go along with them, though I could have afforded more because I was doing a bit of writing at the time — for *Titbits, Answers* and so on. After a while some of the Yorkshire fellows, two miners — they thought, 'What about a bit of cheese . . .' They called it the Shinwell High Tea, and then we found that quite a lot of people wanted to join in. That corner went on for several years — must have gone on until the Second World War.

Hard Times

When I was first an MP, on £400, if I wanted to go home I had to pay my own fare — third class. I had to live in London and keep things going in Glasgow. The only way I could do that was I had a retainer from my union: otherwise, I couldn't have done it. You know this? This is a fact: we had some of our Scottish Members who were suffering from malnutrition.

* * *

J.D. "Isn't there a danger that if you pay MPs too well, you'll get in the wrong sort of people — who are in it mainly for the money?"
It's not so much that. The danger is — some of them aren't worth tuppence!

Personal History

Into Parliament

Before leaving for London, several colleagues and I [from the 17 Scottish Labour MPs returned at the 1922 election] asked the headquarters of the ILP to seek accommodation for us. George Hardie, brother of Keir Hardie, and I were able to find lodgings in Pimlico. Two rooms were available, one at a guinea (105p) weekly and the other at 15s (75p). Being younger than Hardie, I suggested I occupy the smaller room but would share the cost of the two rooms with him. When, owing to inability to provide the fare to return home, we had to remain in London at the weekend, we had to seek food at the most dingy restaurants.

* * *

During the third day [of the new session] I made my maiden

speech. Frankly, I thought little of it. I read *The Times* report on the proceedings and, to my surprise, after referring to speakers from the Labour benches who had failed conspicuously to impress, they added: 'Most of them were more sound and fury than solid debating material. Only Mr Shinwell, the Linlithgow victor, made his mark as a political personality seriously to be considered.'

Prime Ministers

I have known — except the Marquess of Salisbury and Campbell Bannerman — every Prime Minister from the beginning of the century, beginning with Balfour, who was a nephew of the Marquess, until Mrs Thatcher.

I have found my assessment of the character of some of them has been confirmed very often by other people in their writings. Take one example.

Bonar Law

I found him very interesting. Very few people, in the early days and during the time he was operating as a politician and Prime Minister, thought he was of any consequence — a non-leader. I had a different view about him and his debating quality. I found people writing [later] about him confirmed my view that he was far abler than his first appearances demonstrated.

J.D. "He seems to have made very little impact on history. Some PMs, regardless of their character, made impact on history. Others, admirable in various ways, are simply forgotten."
You raise a very interesting point — because I've discovered, by reading carefully, these personalities [PMs] were much abler than the public believed.

J.D. "People who have little interest in politics at all know quite a lot about Disraeli — but nothing about Gladstone who was incomparably a more important political figure. But Disraeli has the charisma and is familiar to people who can't name more than three Prime Ministers."

* * *

It was quite common [in former times] to have a politician's photograph on the wall of a home. That reminds me: only the other day I received a letter from someone saying nothing would please him better than to have my photograph on his wall.

J.D. "I'm a bit of cynic. I'm sure he's going to put it on his wall, but I suggest he's got a whole collection — I hesitate to use the term Rogues' Gallery in your presence — of political photographs."
So that's just one of them. I was hoping you were going to say it was because he admired me more than anyone else!
   Manny laughed heartily. The whisky bottle was passed and we forgot about Prime Ministers and politicians, for the time being.

* * *

J.D. "It's peculiar that three pretty important Premiers were pipe-smokers: Baldwin, Attlee, Wilson.'
That's perfectly true. *Manny reached for his own pipe. I re-lit mine.*

* * *

Stanley Baldwin
As Parliamentary Secretary to the Board of Trade, no one thought he was going to be anything at all. Unobtrusive — we knew him as an industrialist — generous — he gave a great deal of his wealth to the State . . . Then he became Prime Minister — and as Prime Minister I think he was second only to Macmillan. He was also very generous in an individual capacity; also friendly. I met him in the lobby and he said to me, 'Hey, you! you think I'm an encyclopedia?' I said, 'What do you mean?' 'You're always asking me questions.' I said, 'I don't get very good answers.'
   His method of speaking was strange. He had bits of paper, and when he'd made a point he'd take that bit of paper and throw it down. Then he'd go on with another piece of paper, and throw that away.

Neville Chamberlain
I couldn't get to like Chamberlain, although I recognized he was a man of character, and he'd done excellent work [in local government].

Sir Anthony Eden (Lord Avon)

Anthony was in some respects a bit weak. He was a very good Foreign Secretary — no doubt of that. He changed right over. At one time, when we were both in the House of Commons, I would go for him and he would attack me. But we became very friendly. *Manny expressed profound admiration for the present Lord Avon.*

Sir Alec Douglas Home (Lord Home)

He wasn't a great Prime Minister, but he is the The Gentleman of Politics — in style and behaviour — a friendly type. He's an exception.

* * *

I was able to make friends with people like Anthony Eden quite easily — Douglas Home — people like that — Monty. Douglas Home didn't want to be Prime Minister. He was quite content with what he was. I would regard him as a very good Foreign Secretary and describe him as a gentleman–statesman.

Edward Heath

. . . Too fixed in his ideas, too fixed.

J.D. "I never thought of Heath as being a true Conservative."
He wasn't a Tory of the old line. He didn't belong to that company, wasn't accepted as such. Heath was not 'county'.

. . . His fatal mistake wasn't the Common Market. It was facing up to the miners. Why didn't he consult me? I would have told him not to be so stupid. Let them have their own way — you'll catch them some other day!

I think I could get on all right with Heath.

Of Premiers

MacDonald depended on Jimmy Thomas [the popular personality whose career ended in financial disgrace]; Attlee depended on Ernie Bevin, and Wilson depended on Frank Cousins. They [Labour Prime Ministers] always had a trade union leader supporting them.

* * *

British Prime Ministers, weak as some have been, compare favourably with American Presidents.

See also: CALLAGHAN, CHURCHILL, MACDONALD, MACMILLAN, THATCHER, WILSON.

Personal History

A Bad Period

After early successes, 1931 saw Manny out of Parliament and out of a job.

The financial situation was precarious. Then Henderson [General Secretary of the Labour party] suggested I might undertake propaganda activities. All he could offer was £250 annually: any expenses must be met by local constituencies or myself.

From 1931 to 1935 I would address anything from five to eight meetings every week.

Sometimes I'd be asked to stay at the house of some wealthy member of the party. That was the most embarrassing situation of all, because one was really treated like one of the servants. I made up my mind after some of these experiences that I wouldn't accept hospitality again: I'd go to the most dingy hotel.

* * *

As far as my family was concerned . . . they did everything possible to ease my situation. On one occasion I was asked to undertake several meetings in South Wales. By the time I reached Newport I'd spent nearly every penny I had. In the morning, I had no money to pay the hotel bill. I had hoped that because the Secretary [of the local Labour Party] was an old friend, I could speak to him about expenses. He had gone to London. I had enough money to send a telegram to my wife to send two pounds. Eventually, as there seemed no reply forthcoming, I went to look for a place where I could pawn my overcoat. However, not being acquainted with the town, I looked for the three brass balls in vain. I decided to return to the hotel and seek compassion from the receptionist. On the way back, however, I saw a telegraph boy dawdling. I followed him . . . he made his way to the hotel and there was a telegraph note for two pounds.

Racial Problems

At the time of our conversations, Britain's racial problems were epitomized by the comparatively local Brixton riots and the ensuing Scarman Report, but I employed it to lead Manny to talk about broader aspects of this important subject. I gave the personal view that the Scarman Report was "very unrealistic: trendy platitudes, most of it".

I'm not too happy about it myself. What troubles me about it . . . when it was raised in Parliament, if I'd wanted to say anything, I'd have said [we should] provide a new form of training for the police, provide homes for the homeless amongst the coloured people — new housing — and to ensure many of them would have employment . . .

J.D. "Who's going to employ them?"
. . . to be trained. How much is it going to cost? Nobody asked that question. That's what I intended to say, but I thought I'd better leave it, because there are good intentions there . . .

J.D. "Hell's pavement."
. . . but how to implement them's another matter. What Scarman wants would cost three or four hundred million. Where's it coming from?

J.D. "Would it do any good anyway?"
Why do you say that?

J.D. "Because I don't believe there's any point in training black people — for what occupations? There's nothing available, and most people don't want to employ them . . . [A certain amount of devil's advocacy to stimulate answers]. Dangers of lumping all coloured peoples as if they were racially and culturally similar; how can a Black be defined, even if desirable to do so; what about half-castes; where do the Chinese fit in; how could 'positive discrimination' work without being discriminatory?"
On this subject one suffers from a conflict of emotions. Naturally, to those of us who believe we're civilized, anything in the form of discrimination is objectionable, obnoxious. The mere existence of someone of a different colour should not raise any objection in the mind, nor any opposition. That is the ideal.

But one DOES discriminate, whether in private or public. That is obvious. But it operates in a rather strange way. For example, our attitude towards Pakistanis, the Asians and Indians, is less objectionable than it is about Blacks. The Asians and Indians were one time part of the Commonwealth, and also they've become prosperous by their own efforts. They seem to be better off: they work harder. Whereas in the case of the Blacks, they sometimes find it difficult to assimilate. The Asians don't, although their religion is very different. [*This is contrary to conventional opinion: interpretation of the nebulous "facts" of this controversial topic tend to be individualistic, not to say idiosyncratic.*]

J.D. "Yet the Blacks, most of them, were brought up in English-speaking countries."
Immigration has to be controlled. If one considers the [estimated] increase in population of the coloured people in this country in the next few years — twenty years — unless there is housing provision and employment provision, the position will become impossible to control, impossible.

The danger we face is this: if we appear to be discriminating, we're condemned as racialists, when in fact we don't feel that way at all. Why should we feel any hostility to someone of a different colour? Only if their behaviour is bad. Sometimes, when I've used public transport, when I've watched Black people acting in a certain fashion, I've felt troubled about it. I didn't feel I wanted to do anything foolish or unlawful, but sometimes I disliked what I saw. Now, what is one to do about that?

The Option of Repatriation
Are we to reach a situation where the problem is so acute, so difficult to disentangle, that we have to provide facilities to enable many of these people to go back to their own countries? Because by that time it will be almost impossible to arrange anything. What are we faced with then? Despite what Scarman said, you can't stop rioting [entirely] unless you give the coloured people ALL they want. And we're unable to give them all they want. That's putting it very plainly, very simply.

J.D. "The word 'give' is rather important — because a lot of people would ask, why should we GIVE them anything beyond what we're giving what we call 'our own people' for want of a better description. They [the Blacks] appear to be asking for MORE than the white citizen is getting. That's what riles people: 'We want things BECAUSE we're Black.'"
Doesn't it amount to this? We can debate and debate . . . but how WILL the problem be solved?

J.D. "Must one consider the 'Powell Option'?"
Repatriation.

J.D. "But not necessarily voluntary."
Then suppose, in the case of the West Indians, they return and find no

employment . . . what do we do? We've got to provide aid, finance to
that area!

Socialism

What IS Socialism?

How do you define it? To change methods of selecting [Labour Party]
leaders has nothing to do with Socialism. Re-selection of Members has
nothing to do with Socialism. The creation of shadow cabinets, elimina-
tion of certain extreme elements, have nothing to do with Socialism.
What DO we mean by it? For many people — and indeed for the Labour
Party — it means nationalization of the means of production, distribution and exchange. That is the policy — Clause 4 — decided on in
1918.

But that is not enough, because we have discovered that nationalization of that [traditional] kind — the mechanisation of industry — is not
enough because another government comes in and destroys it at once. It
would be very difficult to build it up again.

Now that should be the objective of the Labour Party — to stand by
the Socialist principles, and I would extend them to allow workers to
take part in the administration of industry, its organization, and to be
better informed on its finances . . .

*Manny digressed into the way in which financiers bedevilled one with
technicalities.*

*J.D. "Will they [Labour members] ever agree though [about what
Socialism is]? Healey would say he's a good Socialist. Benn would say
he's a good Socialist. They scarcely seem to belong to the same party, do
they?"*

It's got nothing to do with extremes. What we want is to create a
higher standard of living in a civilized community, to eliminate waste, to
use our resources wisely, and to ensure that what we desire for ourselves
be made available to other countries, particularly those suffering from
malnutrition and impoverishment in the worst forms. That's what I
mean by Socialism. [But] I reject communism.

Strikes

Though partly overtaken by events, these views retain much relevance.

J.D. "Do you think there should be a ballot or just a show of hands [before a strike is called]?"

I'm not sure about it. After all, if a ballot is legalized [as a compulsory measure], preceding a possible strike, then, in effect, you are accepting the right of people to strike. That does exist. If no strike could take place without a ballot, it would mean innumerable ballots. What sort of strike would be affected? Would it just be over a few men who decided to go on strike? Would you have a ballot about that — a ballot which would take weeks? Meanwhile, what's going to happen? Are they going to be out? That's one of the difficulties; you can never be sure of its being expedited to enable a decision to be reached. It may take weeks, even months, if there were complicated issues involved . . . You could have all sorts of trouble and the trouble would last very much longer. And besides, there's nothing to prevent a body of workers on the shop-floor, or any part of any industry, from withdrawing their labour while the ballot is proceeding, justifiably or not. I can understand a ballot being taken if there's a possibility of its being expedited — perhaps in the course of a few days. It's a very expensive business. In the case of Leyland, fifty to sixty thousand men — everyone has to receive a ballot paper. It's got to be prepared, printed, distributed . . . who's going to be responsible for the cost involved? And then, a decision is reached — and suppose the decision is of a very marginal character — a matter of a dozen votes out of a hundred thousand — then the minority would say, 'We haven't really been defeated. Our action has been justified.' All that has to be taken into account. My view is there's been far too much [talk] in support of the case for a ballot, simply because of [public] opposition to trade union actions.

A much better way, of course, would be to provide for arbitration, before [strike] action is taken. For example, if a union intimates to the employers concerned that the workers are dissatisfied with the situation, have put in a demand which has been rejected [then there should be arbitration]. *Manny's argument here became somewhat diffused, but the tenor was that he would like to see arbitration replace confrontation, though there was the problem that, barring compulsory acceptance, an arbitration decision could be rejected by either side.*

J.D. "For true arbitration, the two sides must agree to agree to a decision by the arbitrator."

How are you going to introduce that by legislation? Very difficult indeed. [*The conversation became rather convoluted.*]

Far better to leave things as they are, though there are some things which need to be done: no strike when the security of the nation is involved. That's the first priority. No question of withdrawal of labour where patients in hospitals are likely to be affected adversely . . . where food supplies are going to be curtailed or not distributed at all. Those are essential in what I call a civilized society. On the other hand, we can't prevent a body of workers from withdrawing their labour in a society which believes in competition . . .

* * *

If we have a government more concerned with consensus than confrontation, we'd have some method of arbitration. We've got ACAS, but it hasn't got compulsory powers . . . I think we ought to inject compulsion into industrial relations.

Personal History

The Journalist

During my tour of North Wales [as propagandist for Labour], I was staying in a small hotel near Blaenau Ffestiniog. I decided to go for a long walk. I came to a tiny village. I noticed there was a cobbler's shop, and my shoes were in need of repair. He agreed to repair them while I waited, and as he did so he told me that in the surrounding hills gold had been found, and though the hills were no longer worked for gold, Queen Alexandra's wedding ring had been made from the area's gold. When I returned to my hotel, I wrote a short piece. I sent it to the *Liverpool Post* and received a very useful five pounds.

When I returned from my tours, I had to face unpaid accounts. This meant a stint at the typewriter rushing off a few articles, mainly to popular periodicals like *Answers, Titbits, John Bull*, and also several for the *Daily Herald*.

* * *

A decade later: As it happened, it [not taking an official post during the war] didn't do me any harm. Because I remained out of government, I did an awful lot of articles and made a lot of money out of them — enough to buy a house in Hampstead Garden Suburb.

Manny returned to the House of Commons in 1935. Thereafter he was at the centre of national or party politics, as Minister or Front Bench spokesman: public affairs eclipsed personal history.

Margaret Thatcher

J.D. "What's your attitude to women in politics?"
In my last book I referred to some of them — but not much. I didn't want to say too much because my popularity was fading anyway, and I didn't want to take any chances! I referred to Baroness Tweedsmuir — charming, the most able woman in the House. And I referred to Margaret Thatcher as friendly and capable, but perhaps not firm enough to take on the tasks allotted her. *Before anyone gasps at that assessment, made before she was Prime Minister and several years pre-Falkland Islands war, let us record a change of opinion. Manny next said he now found Mrs Thatcher . . . able and pleasant —* TOO *firm!*

Manny obviously had enjoyed social meetings with Mrs Thatcher. He compared her (first) premiership favourably with Edward Heath's government. I could not incite much interest: Manny was more concerned with past Premiers — even future ones — than the current occupant of Number Ten.

I think that, under the circumstances, having regard to the people about her, close colleagues, and the fact that she's a woman, she's done better than could be expected.

I don't know anyone in the party could have done any better.

An Assessment
Almost at the end of our meetings, I came back to Mrs Thatcher. As mentioned above, Manny had referred to her in a book some years previously. I had to press him to obtain any addition to the few words already quoted. I think his further comments well worth recording,

though it should be re-emphasized that they were made during Mrs Thatcher's first Premiership.

I don't want to be hypercritical in any way — but everybody to his taste. That's the only way I can put it.

Margaret Thatcher: a momentous occasion when a woman MP becomes PM. It's an outstanding event. I express myself quite honestly, and I say this: one has to have a certain sympathy for her at a time like this. She probably didn't know what she was in for. She probably didn't know we were going to face a recession. It takes courage. It takes endurance. Quite frankly, on that ground she's not a person who's a target for criticism. She's a target for criticism on the ground that she and her government have a monetarist policy. She has fixed ideas on that, which is a mistake. If you're PM, you've got to adapt yourself. You've got to be ready for compromise. And if you've got the capacity to compromise, without giving too much away . . . that's her mistake, that's the fatal thing [*by implication, a reluctance to compromise.*]

Finally, about her — the fact that she's occasionally said something about the unemployed — naturally, she's got to be concerned — talking that people should GET work — people should do this and that and get work — she appears unconscious of what it really means to be unemployed. You see, it's probably difficult for her to understand it — it's difficult for many people — you've got to be unemployed yourself to understand it. But when people reach the age of 50, 55 or 60 and have been employed for many years — [then] suddenly [they] lose their employment, and realize after a while they're never going to work again . . . it's not only desperation, it's despair.

It might have done more good if she'd been quite frank, and said, 'I recognize there doesn't seem to be any solution.'

I would go so far as to say the Labour Party can no more solve unemployment than Mrs Thatcher can.

* * *

She's surrounded by a number of people [*somewhat diminished in number since*] — they call 'em Wets: I don't like the term at all but I understand it. I've been in governments myself and I know what happens. I know how you can be surrounded by people who are very able, very affable. They will pat you on the back, and would seem to be encouraging you, will offer you a drink or invite you to stay in their country houses — and would cut your throat behind your back. *An interesting form of political assassination.*

Trade Unions

At the beginning of the century, the trade unions decided they must have parliamentary representation. They met at the Memorial Hall in Farringdon Street [London] for that purpose. An attempt was made by some of the Socialists present, like Ben Tillett, trade union leader, and Keir Hardie, political leader of the Independent Labour Party, to create a working-class Labour Party. That was rejected. The trade union delegates made it quite clear they were not concerned with these matters. They were concerned with one thing, and one thing only — to put an end to anti-trade union legislation, to make it possible for trade unions to operate legally and, for that purpose, to obtain Parliamentary representation. That alone was their purpose.

Now, as the years go by, they obtain moderate success. Then, because of legislation brought in by Baldwin [after the 1926 General Strike], and then by other Prime Ministers and so on, the trade unions were faced by barriers, obstacles, boundaries . . . This called for political action, and that is why there was a change in trade union policy — no longer industrial in character, but political. And therefore they supported the Labour Party, to obtain the benefits they had failed to gain by themselves, to have politicians fighting for them in the House of Commons.

More years go by, and the unions become powerful — mighty powerful — so all-powerful that they incur displeasure even of some of their friends — too powerful — doing things that never ought to be done, were never envisaged by the pioneers of the trade union movement.

What a Change

Again there comes unemployment. What a change! Trade union funds disappearing, vanishing almost. Trade union treasurers in difficulties, not knowing how to get through with miserable contributions; vast numbers no longer paying contributions; salaries going up all the time — all the rest of it — until they begin to wonder whether it's worth-while to be associated with the Labour Party. Len Murray, as secretary of the TUC, said in effect: 'Unless we can be assured the Labour Party is going to be united and is going to produce another government, we'll have to consider whether it's worth being associated.' That's what he said.

Don't forget that in the 1920s some of the trade union leaders, a few of them, decided to form a Trade Union Labour Party. They were scotched by Arthur Henderson, but it nearly succeeded, and there've been occasions when trade union leaders have blamed the politicians and said, 'You've failed. You're no use to us at all.' And this is why some of them, like Scargill and company, adopt the syndicalist attitude and say, 'It's got to be fought out on the streets.' That's what they mean.

An Incomes Policy

I am in favour of arbitration [See STRIKES] I would go further: I would have an incomes policy. I've presented it to the Cabinet on two occasions. I've advocated these things.

When the unions were at the top of their form, when there was full employment, they did as they damn well liked . . . Do you think unemployment has changed their minds? Of course it has. Perhaps not so much unemployment itself as dealing with the facts . . . They don't know where the money's going to come from.

The TUC is practically bankrupt. In order to undertake certain propositions that have been talked about, the unions require an enormous amount of money — money that is now devoted to pension funds.

I'm in favour of trade unions. I believe we've got to have some form of protection from unprincipled employers, and that was the whole purpose at the beginning — Tolpuddle Martyrs, all that sort of thing . . . I've been through it myself, so I understand, but I agree with Lord Acton, 'Too much power is going a bit too far' — I can't quote it as accurately as I used to be able to. Some of the things that have been done about ambulances and hospitals . . . how can one support them doing that? Nobody's going to tell me that made a contribution to the progress of trade unions.

* * *

Collective bargaining never produced anything worth-while. Extraordinary thing is this: The trade union leaders and the Labour Party object to the operation of market forces, don't they? They're always saying market forces are the cause of trouble. But when it comes to trade unions [in operation] it IS market force that operates — market force all the time. It's the strong who decide, the muscle decides, until the crunch comes — and it'll come with the miners if they aren't careful.

Prospects of Civil War

The present government have used their powers for the purpose of destroying nationalizaton, public ownership — and they're doing more of it. Suppose that goes on and at the next election the Conservatives get back again [as they did with a huge majority] and you've got to wait five years — maybe into the next century! — before Labour is strong enough and people with Socialist ideas come to power . . .

What occurs to me is this: sooner or later, what we call the reactionaries — the reactionary elements in society who control society to a considerable degree — they are confronted by people who say, 'We've had enough of this — and if we can't by Parliamentary means gain what we want . . .' Isn't it likely we will get an extreme form of opposition that will lead to civil war?

Take this possibility. What if, for example, the trade union movement comes to the conclusion it can't get very much through the Labour Party. They have been financing the Labour Party; they built the Labour Party. What are they going to do? Work with the Conservative government? With an SDP [Alliance] party if it came to power? And you get the same answer as you do all the time — you have strikes . . .
Manny indicated the possibility of a breakdown of our industrial society, a comparatively rare expression of despair from a normallly sanguine temperament.

Lust for Power
J.D. "Some trade unions are very reactionary, in the way the old Guilds were."
. . . you mentioned [on another occasion] the lust for power. That affects the trade unions as much as anyone. Their leaders have power over vast numbers of men. And if they decided one day to merge, they'd have enormous power — and they might use it to the detriment of the whole country. What are the trade union leaders out for?

J.D. "Power."
They've got more than power. They've got wealth, too.

Personal History

Marriage

My first wife [Fay] was a wonderful person. We lived together for fifty-one years.

I married again — for thirteen years, until she died: [Dinah], a highly intelligent woman.

I then married again [Sarah] — shouldn't have — out of compassion — the widow of an old friend.

They all died of cancer — never a divorce, never a separation.

After the death of my third wife, I lived on my own — did my own cooking. I moved here [the house of daughter Lucy and her husband, Manny Stern] in September 1979.

*   *   *

We leave Manny's Personal History — a few facets of so many experiences — with him ensconced in the tranquillity of his London home, not that far in miles, but an age apart, from the site of Freeman Street, Spitalfields, where he was born a hundred years ago.

War and Peace

The Germans have had enough of war. They fought it out with the Russians and got the worst of it. The Russians consider the Germans their number one priority enemy. Nothing would give the Russians more pleasure than to destroy the Germans. They partly destroyed them by carving up the country into two units.

An Arrangement With Russia?

In an atomic war who will strike first? The Russians have got targets all listed in this country, in America and elsewhere . . . all they need to do is push the button — and devastation everywhere. Then there's a measure of retaliation, and we've got nuclear war.

You get a hundred thousand people protesting in London against nuclear armaments. It may be they're not only protesting against that: they're protesting against war at all — don't want any war.

J.D. "The equivalent of the peace movement before the last war . . ."
. . . and maybe this peace movement is against war of any kind — even to the extent of |the protesters| being prepared to come to some arrangment with the Russians. Suppose the Russians came along to the SALT talks and all that — damned nonsense even with verification — and suppose they made an offer, not to America but to the Germans, to the British, saying, 'We don't want war at all. Let's come to some arrangement.' Don't you think that would be acceptable to a vast number of people in Britian, in Germany, Belgium, Holland, Norway, Sweden, Denmark? Of course it would be. Now the Russians might be in that situation |of wanting to make serious proposals| because of their food problems. They have great |agricultural| difficulties. Suppose that happens.

J.D. "What would they be offering that would be acceptable? What would prove irresistible to Europeans?"
You may think this stupid of me: I'll take my chance. I don't think the Russians need offer more than to make an outright declaration, 'We don't want war in Europe and we haven't the slightest intention of doing anything in that direction. And we are prepared to sit down and discuss with you not only control of conventional armaments but their abolition.'

J.D. "Would you believe them?"
You're asking me! I've only got to read what they're doing to the dissidents . . . Not me!

J.D. "People believe what they want to believe. They'd want to believe that."

* * *

Continuing Stalemate
Can you envisage another twenty-five, thirty, fifty years of the Cold War?

J.D. "Yes, I can."

You've got the armaments, the nuclear stuff all ready. And we do nothing for a long period, and during that time [there are] demonstrations, peace-loving people passing resolutions, governments not quite sure of themselves, not spending any more money on defence. Isn't that a possibility — a condition of stalemate?

J.D. "Stalemate is what preserves the peace. Any form of peace is a stalemate historically, unless you have one dominant power. The Pax Britannica lasted virtually from Waterloo to the Somme. Though plenty of fighting, no major wars. That was through the dominance of Britain. Short of that kind of situation anything is a compromise, because no one side feels quite strong enough to do anything about it . . ."

. . . Are we certain that a war could occur, whether conventional or nuclear, unless the Soviet Union commits some act which the West could not accept — invasion of some country? They've already invaded Afghanistan and not created the confrontation one might have expected. Unless that happens, one can look forward . . . we might have the next forty to fifty years of stalemate, when all the munitions we produce are of no value at all. A strong possibility.

I don't want to indulge in pacifist talk: I'm not that way. I don't feel that way, and certainly not about the Russians. On the other hand . . . even without the use of nuclear weapons, using missiles — long-range and all the rest — in a conventional war we're bound to use some strategic weapons. That's why we've got them.

J.D. "Are we, because we're Europeans — though the British don't like being called Europeans — over-concentrating on European defence? Isn't Russia really more interested in the Middle East? What does Russia want in Europe? She has her 'cordon sanitaire' of satellite states."

I've always thought if there was any [major] trouble at all, it would be in the Middle East. How often have I said — many times in the Commons and in the Lords — that the Russians don't want war. They don't need it: they get all they want without war . . .

If this pacifist movement develops — you might almost say world-wide — we have to consider the effect on the production of munitions, sales of arms by one country to another, and the effect on industrial production and our financial situation.

J.D. "We're a big exporter of arms . . ."

I think we might consider that. Suppose we're spending £11,000 million now on armaments and organization. Supposing there were a strong feeling — a Labour government came in and was powerful enough to win support of public opinion to reduce expenditure by, say, £2,000 million. Now the country would like it because it would mean a reduction in taxation — more for investment in industry, new machine tools, etc. Suppose you had a situation like that — it could happen in the next five to six years. [*This was before Kinnock, as new leader of the Labour Party, intimated that he might favour an actual increase in expenditure on conventional forces.*] The armaments industry would be gradually reduced. How long would it be before the Russians realized that their vast manpower and industrial potential would allow their country to develop, with the aid of Western finance?

All these demonstrations are futile and irrelevant to the situation.

To condense Manny's summation: If the Russians decide, because of their agricultural difficulties and a desire to produce more for their people, to become more civilized — even democratic . . . if they decided to adopt that attitude, what an effect it would have on the world!

* * *

J.D. "If you have the disarmament some people go for, and if everyone does disarm, what on earth happens to enormous industries that make these things? Are they going to make bath-tubs and TV sets? They can't: there are too many already. The Russians would benefit most, of course, because they could do with more bath-tubs and TVs. The Americans would be in a pretty bad way if they hadn't got an armaments industry." [*This was a long, sometimes rambling conversation, here audibly punctuated by the sounds of whisky glasses being replenished.*]

In order to provide employment for people, we must talk about the possibility of war?

J.D. "One good thing about the armaments industry is that half of them become pretty swiftly obsolete and therefore are chucked away, or sold second-hand, and you've got a second generation [of weapons] coming along . . . You should know."

We're doing that with our warships . . .

J.D. ". . . and that's good for the economy, isnt' it? An awful lot of people — how many people do you think are employed, in the broadest sense, just in our own armaments industry?"

It runs into thousands — into thousands. This expenditure is becoming so vast, insupportable. You reach a point where you can no longer bear it. We must say it's got to stop, we've got to reduce it, we're prepared to say to the Americans, 'Don't make any trouble for us.'

We never did arrive at any conclusions; the topic was too wide.

Could Satellite States Weaken?

It is difficult to envisage what a possible aggressor is likely to do . . . because of that there is so much uncertainty, insecurity, which includes waste . . . We have vast numbers of men who are not engaged in warfare [although concerned with the armed forces] and who never have to be involved. . . . The Russians have indulged in huge expenditure, in excess of what they require even if they do fear aggression or what they require in practice if they were involved [in major war].

The more we can attract the satellites from their association with Russia . . . the more likely there is to be ultimate peace.

J.D. "The East Germans appear to be extremely hard line pro-Moscow."
That would appear to be so on the surface, but I very much doubt if it applies to the East German population in general, for the conditions under which they were living for many years were very harsh.

J.D. "But they're much better off now through their industrial success."
I had the opportunity of visiting East Germany, when they were kind enough to allow me to visit barracks, the depots — some of them. Usually they don't do that. They probably suspected that, though not on their side, I was anxious to encourage them in some form. What I wanted to do at the time — before they were completely involved — [was to see if] it might be possible to weaken the [Russian] connection. It hasn't happened.

* * *

I think it is important to clarify those subjects concerned with nuclear weapons. A 'nuclear-free zone' cannot be unilateral; must be multi-lateral. Labour muddled the issue. How can you be unilateral and yet support NATO?

On Cruise missiles, I consider two views, which are contradictory. Purely from a defence point of view, I think they might be very useful [situated in this country]. The other point is that I doubt whether they'd be fully effective for their purpose: they're not particularly mobile. There is so much confusion about their usefulness.

It is difficult to come to a conclusion about any weapon, in my experience, until it has been used in some form. I would say that about all weapons. What appears to be the best weapon in the world — unless it has been PROVED to be effective, it's better to be cautious.

Harold Wilson (Lord Wilson of Rievaulx)

In the case of Wilson, when I was chairman of the Parliamentary Labour Party, yes [I got on with him]. But after I resigned, No — no more.

J.D. "Did he become antagonistic?"
He didn't become antagonistic to me. But I became a bit antagonistic to him, by saying the man was very capable, very competent, a good debater, but lacked a coherent sense of direction — didn't know where he was going.

J.D. "He rather prided himself on going with the wind — pragmatism was his word."
That's another thing I didn't like about him. Look what he did with Wigg! [*the late Lord (George) Wigg, a great friend of Manny's.*] No one backed him more than Wigg. Wigg could have destroyed him, but he didn't.

There was an occasion when he appointed me as one of a select group on the D-Notices Committee [of Privy Councillors]. Lord Radcliffe was chairman and Selwyn Lloyd represented the Conservatives and I represented Labour. I met Chapman Pincher [the celebrated investigative journalist] and he said, 'I haven't seen you for a long time. Do you remember the D-Notices Committee?' *The Premier, Wilson, had accused the* Daily Express *(Chapman's paper at the time) of publishing information in alleged contravention of a D-Notice, a form of covert press censorship accepted by editors. The* Express *rejected the accusation.* I remember questioning Chapman Pincher like a barrister. I questioned the Permanent Secretary at the Foreign Office. I questioned everybody, so that Lord Radcliffe was a bit worried about it. Why appoint me to the Committee? Anyway, I did it, and then we had to make a report — and Wilson thought I was going to report in his favour after he'd appointed me. Nothing of the sort.

119

I made my speech in the House of Commons on the basis of the report. To the surprise of everybody, I took a very objective view. I gave credit to the witnesses. I scrutinized all the evidence, and I came to the conclusion it was a mistake to [prosecute] Express Newspapers although I didn't like what they did. What Wilson wanted: he wanted me to come down on his side. How do I know that? I don't want to make it public at this stage, but I knew that. I was told about it.

* * *

Wilson's very good at giving someone a nudge and saying, 'Have you heard so-and-so' — concerning someone. Very good at that.

Manny came back to what he obviously considered Wilson's shabby treatment of George Wigg, but without specifying its nature, merely saying:

He used Wigg. Without Wigg he would never have got in . . . and then — [*a click of the fingers.*] That sort of thing I dislike.

J.D. "Isn't that part of politics?"
Well, you can have it . . . I had enough of him. I don't think anyone, apart from Wigg, could have served him better than I did. I kept him going at a time when he only had a majority of three — until I said, 'I've had enough. I'm going to resign.' He said, 'That'll be a disaster.' And he said at a reception in Downing Street, on another occasion — he referred to what I had done to keep the party going. In fact, there's been mostly trouble ever since: since then there's been trouble all the time. But while that government was in, I kept them like that — *a gesture of the thumb denoting complete control.*

Yet There Is Hope (Tape 22 (b))

It was purely coincidental — in no way planned — that extracts from this last tape of my conversations with Manny should form an apt finale. I've asked myself, will ever a time come when these sectarian conflicts no longer exist? We have so many of them — Christianity, Judaism,

Islam, Buddhism, a great variety . . . Will ever a time come when all of them accept the Almighty as the creator of the universe — God, Allah, Jahveh — the beginning and the ultimate?

J.D. "There are a vast number of people who don't believe in a single deity. Monotheism is by no means universal."

Would it not be admitted that sectarianism creates conflict? And continues to create conflict, in Ireland, in the Middle East — conflict. Are we to understand that so long as there's this sectarian attitude — differences in religions and attitudes to the Almighty — as long as these exist there will be conflict? We can never hope to eradicate conflict from society until we have abolished sectarianism? I don't know.

J.D. "Sectarianism is on the increase. There are more sects — some quite big — than there were only fifty years ago."

But I want an answer to my question: is conflict to continue as long as there's sectarianism?

J.D. "I believe human beings always fight each other. It's a peculiar feature of the human animal — unlike any other — that it will kill its own kind for no particular reason."

Yes, there'll always be conflict. But is conflict always associated with sectarianism? You can have conflict [for umpteen reasons]. I recognize that: I don't object to that. But are we to understand that because there are differences between people about religion, theology, that means conflict is going to continue for ever and ever, Amen?

J.D. "In my view, yes."

Are we then to be satisfied that civilization in those circumstances is impossible?

J.D. "Mankind has been on this planet for such a very short time — and it's my belief it won't last very long."

What?

J.D. "Mankind. Shall we say, in twenty thousand years — fifty thousand — it's more than likely that the human race will have disappeared and the world will be able to be the good place it was before man developed."

Why should you envisage that situation? What's the justification?

*J.D. "Because I think mankind is almost determined to destroy itself —
which no other species has ever thought. Other species have disappeared,
but not of their own volition."*

What's the determining factor in this self-destruction?

*J.D. "I think it is in-built in human psychology. It starts off with killing
each other, but it'll come to such a peak that for one reason or another
— may be disease, may be over-development of the brain — [the human
race will self-destruct]."*

I agree, on reflection, when one indulges in deep thinking, meditation
about the future, it is very difficult to believe the world population will
continue for ever in its present form. But on the other hand, there is no
reason to assume we'll ever vanish. What is by no means unlikely is that
as a result of physical, natural changes — earthquakes, geological
changes — the supremacy of water over land — that what we know as
humanity may disappear. But there's no reason to suppose that other
civilizations, or supposed civilizations, should not appear.

*J.D. "Perfectly likely. After all, the air-breathing whales and dolphins
were once on land. Might not the highly intelligent dolphin return to the
land if we were not there? They could take over from us — and might
make a better job of it. My reading of history is that the human race has
made a complete hash of the world."*

What Is It All About?
You know, when we talk in this fashion on these things, we're really
asking, 'What is it all about?' Why did it start? Why was it necessary?
With all the conflicts, disputations, all the heartbreaks, all the frustra-
tions, disappointments, all the hopes and expectations unfulfilled —
Why did it begin at all? Wouldn't it be better not for it to have
happened? [*Manny's basic optimism reasserted itself:*] . . . one must
retain some hope, faith — if not faith in others, faith in oneself . . .
making a contribution, doing what he or she thinks best — though what
that best is, is hard to define.

*J.D. "If you have faith in yourself, you go on. If you haven't got faith in
yourself, you might as well commit suicide."*
   Manny was musing: All the books that have been written — what
philosophers have written — what churches have preached — at the
lowest common denominator, the politicians . . . [*Provocatively, I awoke
him —*]

J.D. "When you talk about books — in ten thousand years' time, shall we say, no one will read Shakespeare because no one will be able to read him any more than you or I can read a cuneiform tablet from Assyria."

What a terrible thing for an Englishman to say! That the time will come when we won't be able to read Shakespeare!

J.D. "May be translated into whatever language we're then speaking, but it won't be the words of Shakespeare."

That's the final word! Would you dare say a Scotsman would declare that the time will come when no one will pay any attention to the words of Robbie Burns?

J.D. "He'll have to be a student of ancient languages. As a Sassenach, I can't read Burns today!"

I think we're going too far.

J.D. "We're putting forward some philosophical considerations."

How long do you give this universe of ours?

J.D. "I've been talking about the human race, not the universe."

How long do you give them, the human race? *I rather liked being asked my opinion — something Olympian about it. I thought a rough estimate would do!*

J.D. "I'd say fifty thousand years."

That's a long time.

J.D. "Very short in relation to the cosmic scene."

Do you think there's anything in this theory of reincarnation? Isn't it possible? I could almost give you a clue to it. Karl Marx died in September, 1884 — and I was born in October, 1884! Is that the sort of thing that happens? There are any number of illustrations of that kind.

We discussed aspects of the reincarnation theories, deciding that we did not much favour achieving Nirvana via transmogrification into humble life-forms.

* * *

Manny inquired whether I thought the type of conversation we were having was still possible in 'good society'.

J.D. *"I don't believe most people do a great deal of thinking — very unusual for a politician, that's certain. You're unusual in that respect."*

They're usually thinking of the next election.

I raised again the uproar broadcast as Parliamentary proceedings. I had earlier the same day listened to a recording of what "sounded like a riot in a Comprehensive school".

Isn't it symptomatic? We have it on the football field.

J.D. *"But one doesn't expect the House of Commons to copy the football field."*

Perhaps it's the football field copies the House of Commons!

J.D. *"Maybe the cause of riots on the terraces is because they heard it in the Commons?"*

Let Us Not Be Too Depressed

I was hoping to develop this theory of mine about the universe — it's a very interesting topic — on which one can indulge in a great deal of thought.

J.D. *"I think it's fascinating to talk about it, but it has no practical relevance at all. It is the impractical things that are more interesting than the practical, which may, of course, account for the fact that few practical things are ever done. People are dealing with lovely theories and immense philosophical notions — as we are — but not getting down to practical things, in politics."*

How can we? Look at the situation. Vast unemployment, a great deal of poverty. We've got a prison crisis; we're not on good terms with some other countries; we've got trouble in Ireland . . . and bombing goes on, and gunning goes on — and there you are. And what are we to do about it all? To speak about it, to quarrel about it . . .

J.D. *"There isn't anything particularly new about all this. We've often discussed how history repeats itself. I reckon in 1848, the great revolutionary year, more people were assassinated than in the whole of the current decade. I don't think things have changed all that much —*

except that we now have what it is fashionable to call the media bringing the troubles into the home . . ."

Perhaps we're unduly depressed by prevailing conditions, and ought not to be. After all's said and done, there are a great many features of society that are encouraging. And there is Nature itself to look at, to think about, to explore — books to read, stories to be heard — and, above all, there are the arguments and differences of opinion, honestly expressed.

* * *

So far as recording goes, thus ended our conversations. I have only a few words to add. As I had a final drink with Manny, and we continued to chat about nothing in particular, I was vaguely conscious I had been a privileged person . . .

Postscript

My association with Manny Shinwell was comparatively brief. Yet, in retrospect, I feel it had a depth, an intensity, lacking in many a relationship spread over a longer period. I came into his orbit at a time when he was still unusually active in an elder statesman role in the House of Lords. Not that it ceased after I had stopped visiting him, but his actual participation, as opposed to his interest, in public affairs was to become more selective and his attendances at Westminster naturally less frequent. I caught his attention at the summit of his ultimate career — that of observer, counsellor and remembrancer.

As I said at the beginning of this work, I endeavoured to remain a background figure, the 'voice off', intruding only to spur Manny's reflections and memories. Why was I ever in this position? the reader is entitled to ask. Like most things of importance, it came about by chance.

I had enjoyed some amicable professional contacts with Jeremy Greenwood when he was a rising star in the world of publishing. At a moment when he had gone independent and was establishing his own imprint at his burgeoning Quiller Press, I came fortuitously into his orbit again. Over a pint in a Kensington tavern, he asked me if I would be interested in compiling a fresh type of biographical work on a veteran politician. I was intrigued by the prospect. I had retired from direct employment and had reverted to freelance writing. I had published several books, but they had mostly been on a single speciality: I welcomed the opportunity to re-enter the more general arena of authorship.

With Jeremy, I had an introductory meeting with Manny Shinwell at the House of Lords. Our series of conversations started shortly afterwards. I had absolutely no notion as to what, if any, sort of book would emerge. I am reasonably sure Manny envisaged something quite different to this — something much more a political testament. He would occasionally question me as to how 'the book' was coming along. I must now avow I was evasive: I had not any idea what would finally result from these tens of thousands of recorded words (even allowing that some tapes were not wholly decipherable). I did not immediately set about transcribing and collating them. I had urgent writing assignments, was moving house, and there seemed no urgency: Manny's centenary, to celebrate which the book was planned, lay some time ahead. I am not immune to that author's complaint, procrastination. Then the moment arrived to get down to work, and for weeks I became immersed in playing and re-playing the tapes.

It was fascinating to me to rediscover how my relationship with Manny had developed. Its progress may even be apparent in the differing style of various sections, particularly in the concluding tape 22(b) where it is obvious that we have abandoned politician–interviewer roles and are just two friends putting the universe in perspective! We had, inevitably, commenced fairly formally, but a rapport was very quickly established. More than that, I soon acquired a deepening affection for Manny. It is not hyperbole to describe him as a lovable person. Oddly, this growing attachment was to the detriment of my assignment. I found we were going off in all directions, indulging in cosy chats to our mutual enjoyment but which were of negligible interest to third parties.

There was an additional piquancy to our camaraderie, for me at least. We came from totally disparate backgrounds, yet ones that were strangely complementary. Manny had a strong family grounding, had scant schooling, escaped from poverty and was self-educated. I was an adopted child of obscure origin, was brought up in rich neglect, took no advantage of expensive scholastic facilities, and was self-educated. Manny had started by being jingoistically Tory and soon became a dedicated Socialist. I had played early with Socialistic ideas and become an apolitical Conservative. Manny steadfastly adhered to a belief that principles must finally triumph: I am convinced that self-interest dominates all human activity. We got along famously.

I feel justified in taking a view of Emanuel Shinwell. I enormously respected the fact that I found he had, through all the batterings of political life, retained an idealism intact — almost. Occasional flashes of pessimism were always countered by reiteration of his faith in human nature. When I intruded a note of realism, which some call cynicism, he would usually reject it — with an amused tolerance, as if indulging the folly of the young!

Apart from the word Change — the inevitably of Change — the one he most used to me was Problems. That problems have seemingly multiplied rather than diminished in his unique span of life in public affairs had, I discovered, in no way diminished his certainty that they can be finally solved — by Socialism. Not necessarily the Socialism of the Labour Party: rather, the Socialism of high principle, not dogma. Manny visualized an intensely British, unashamedly patriotic form of Socialism. I could almost agree with a Socialism such as he propounded, with its insistence on adequate national defence and a disbelief in the sort of nuclear disarmament advocated by some who claim to be members of the same party as Manny helped establish.

However, I must confess that when it came to solutions for the problems of which he constantly spoke, Manny did, to my mind, sometimes become the politician. He would propound desirable aims, hint at policies, but when pressed as to their practicability, he could — though criticizing the lack of realism in others — with practised ease disengage and pass on to another subject. I did not respect him the less for this — I admired his agility — but it is a poor chronicler who permits admiration to verge on idolatry.

In his ministerial posts, Manny could be intensely pragmatic; not an adjective he favoured. Yet, I repeat, I must describe him as an idealist. His fundamental hope for the future was as undimmed as he approached his hundredth year as it was when he was agitating for workers' rights in Glasgow at the century's turn. Hopes undimmed, I say, yet I felt his faith in the realization of those hopes had been postponed to some distant era when the almost mystical principles of the Socialism in which he believed have been put to work.

As much as any of us, of any statesman, Manny was capable of uttering pronouncements as predictable as a pundit's answer on BBC radio's "Any Questions". To my mind, this only demonstrated his essential humanity. Naturally, I have excised his most banal statements. On the other hand, I have not gone for the 'Wit and Wisdom of . . .' sort of book which makes out that a person's conversation was solely a parade of epigrams, amusing paradoxes and thought-provoking ideas. Manny's conversations with me were spiced with humour — not the brittle badinage of social small-talk nor the jocularity of the political clown, but the humour of manner and intonation which cannot be reproduced on paper. We did not swap jokes, though many were our shared chuckles.

It may quite correctly be asked, why did I not go back to Manny later, when, say, Mrs Thatcher had formed her second administration? Quite simply, I did not want to. I did not wish for a revision of Manny's views, nor did I feel his sensible remarks concerning, for instance, coal nationalization would be rendered more pertinent by after-thoughts relating to 1984's troubles in the industry. We have not here been running a course in current affairs. Largely we have been dealing with political nostalgia — to epitomize the character and thinking of a single individual. Manny constantly told me of the importance of history, how the past shapes our present: he saw much history enacted.

I think of Manny Shinwell as a great man, a man of blinding honesty despite several generations lived in a world filled with chicanery; a thinker, a worker, one who has helped change the face of Britain. Those are clichés. At least a cliché is neither an exaggeration nor a lie, so let us end with one from Manny: trite it may sound, but it is honest –

> "There are an awful lot of bad things in the world.
> But there are an awful lot of good things."

Outline of Lord Shinwell's career

Born 18th October 1884, Freeman St, Spitalfields

Glasgow: First job, 1896, a tobacco firm's delivery boy at 4 shillings a week.

No regular employment until joined Scottish Co-Op Wholesale Society at age of 25.

In 1903, joined Independent Labour Party.

First general election activity, 1906.

First official position, 1909, as member of Glasgow Trades Council.

Nominated by Council and Garment Workers' Union to committee investigating home-workers' sweated labour (average wages, 5 shillings a week).

Regular visits to London involved: first experience of House of Commons.

1911, seamen's strike, Glasgow Trades Council asked for help, and Manny became secretary of Scottish Seamen's Union.

First World War, employed on work of national importance collecting seamen to man auxiliary naval vessels.

Contested Linlithgow in 1919 general election. Clyde workers demonstrated; Manny arrested, sentenced to 5 months' prison.

Won Parliamentary seat, 1922.

In first Labour (minority) government, 1923, given Mines Department.

Acting in place of Minister of Labour, Manny negotiated good wage increase for miners. Moved to London.

Defeated in 1924 election. Re-elected 1928. Financial Secretary, War Office; soon transferring to Mines Department as Parliamentary Secretary. After negotiations with International Labour Organization in Geneva, achieved agreement for $7\frac{1}{2}$-hour day in all countries, but agreement never ratified.

On Labour party's unemployment committee with Sir Oswald Mosley of whose intentions Manny deeply suspicious.

1931: National Government. Labour seats reduced from 289 to 46. Manny out.

Hard, energetic four years as party propagandist, touring country.

Triumph in 1935 when Manny gained 21,000 majority over his old colleague, former premier Ramsay MacDonald, at Seaham (Durham).

1940: refused official post and business offers; supported war effort in Commons, and became successful in journalism.

After Labour's 1945 victory, as Minister of Fuel and Power saw coal nationalization through. Became Privy Councillor. Ministry downgraded by Attlee; Manny reluctantly accepted Secretaryship of State, War Office. Secretary for War and Minister of Defence 1950–1. Widely acclaimed as brilliant Minister though criticized by own party for supporting two-year conscription.

Lost Seat on Labour Party Executive.

1950–70, sat for Easington Division of Durham.

1964, chairman of Parliamentary Labour Party, too much a disciplinarian for some. Resigned.

1965, made Companion of Honour.

1970, decided not to stand again for Commons seat.

Created Baron Shinwell of Easington and became active member of the Upper House.

Index